Evergreen
FAITH

ISBN: (paperback) 979-8-9878075-0-7
ISBN: (ebook) 979-9-9878075-1-4

Cover design:
Lexi Wright (IG: @lexiwri_illustration)

Edited by:
Megan Tatreau (IG: @purple_pencil_proofing)

First Edition: 2023
10 9 8 7 6 5 4 3 2 1

To my pastor, Eugene McCoy,
upon whose shoulders I stand.

Contents

Acknowledgments

Writing a book is hard. I knew that intuitively; now I really know it. My family has been a stalwart of patience through this entire process. Specifically, I owe my wife, Jennifer a tremendous debt of gratitude for her grace, encouragement, and strength through the entire writing process. She has been an amazing source of inspiration and motivation during those times when I didn't think I would ever finish.

My son, Devin, and daughter-in-law, Lexi, were a consistent breath of fresh air. Their infectious joy as they got engaged and planned their wedding was the perfect distraction for resetting myself whenever I got lost in my own head. Devin, thank you for knowing exactly how to make me laugh and for pushing that button as often as possible. Lexi, thank you joining the family and for lending your amazing talent to the cover design. You both are an incredible blessing, and I can't wait to see where the Lord takes you.

Thank you, as well, to my church family. Your prayers were felt every step of the way, and I am honored to serve shoulder to shoulder with each of you in the Kingdom of God.

Lastly, thank you to my editor, Megan Tatreau, and the cadre of draft readers who endured the many emails and pages of some objectively terrible prose. Your insightful feedback made this book what it is today, and has shaped my own approach to, and style of, writing—I believe for the better.

Now, Father, this book is just words on pages. May the reader holding it receive the particular message You have for them as they read. To You alone go all the glory, all the honor, and all the praise.

Evergreen FAITH

A Study of the Revelation Letters

J.F. Wright

Introduction

The letters to the seven churches are God's x-rays, given to us so that we might examine our own lives and ministries.

– **Warren Wiersbe**

A n evergreen tree is one that remains green throughout the year. Merriam-Webster defines evergreen as "having foliage that remains green and functional through more than one growing season; retaining freshness or interest." Evergreen trees remain green as they weather all sorts of storms and extreme seasons. Recently, the term has been used to define something as "universally and continually relevant," indicating the perennial nature of a particular idea or statement as opposed to one that doesn't age well.[1]

What is evergreen faith? It's faith that retains freshness, relevance, and functionality in all seasons. Evergreen faith doesn't protect people from the storm. Instead, it sees people through the storm, becoming stronger and even more enduring because of it. Evergreen faith remains as society changes, as culture becomes increasingly secular,

---

1   *Merriam-Webster.com Dictionary*, s.v. "evergreen," accessed February 15, 2023, https://www. merriam-webster.com/dictionary/evergreen.

as greed, corruption, and abuse are found in both civil and religious leaders. Evergreen faith is not private faith, but it is personal. It shapes individuals, standing strong and verdant in a spiritually hostile environment.

The night of Jesus's betrayal, He prayed, "I do not ask you to take [My disciples] out of the world, but to keep them from the evil one. As You sent Me into the world, I also have sent them into the world."[2] Jesus never meant for His Church to live and exist separately from the world. Living in holy huddles has never been an option for Christians. The world will always challenge and question our faith. This is not necessarily a bad thing. In fact, it can be a good thing.

Jesus sent His Church into the world to be a spiritual influence on the world. His disciples respond to popular culture the same way He did: by living differently. Many of Jesus's teachings follow a pattern: "You have heard it said...But I say." He taught and lived in a society defined by Jewish and Greco-Roman culture, yet His life and teachings were vastly different from both. He lived in the world but was not of the world, and not once did His faith waiver. Even while He was being executed. That is evergreen faith.

Christians represent Christ's kingdom as its ambassadors and His message carriers. The Church is Jesus's mechanism for conveying the gospel to the world. We're it. There is no other plan. Faith in Jesus as the Son of God is not universally accepted, but it is universally relevant. Somehow, the ways in which we respond to our culture should display Jesus, so that people are drawn to Him. Does the Church always get it right? No, but Christ never gives up on His people. In fact, He promised to never leave them, saying, "I am with you always, even to the end of the age."[3]

---

2   John 17:15, 18.
3   Matthew 28:20.

Seven churches in western Anatolia (Asia Minor, modern day Turkey) received the Revelation written by John, along with letters dictated by Christ. As the final book in the Bible, Revelation represents Jesus's final words to His Church. Typical modern messaging around Revelation focuses on the horrifying images of God's judgment, a years-long global tribulation culminating in an armed conflict between the army of Christ and that of the antichrist. However, Jesus meant for His final words to be a consolation to His Church, comforting His people not only in their current situation, but for every situation they would find themselves in throughout history. John understood this when he wrote, "Blessed is he who reads and those who hear the words of this prophecy and heeds the things which are written in it; for the time is near."[4]

Although those seven churches were relatively close to each other, they represent the Church at large. Each endured similar hardships, temptations, and cultural hostility because of their faith in Jesus. Their responses to the surrounding culture were the topic of Jesus's letters. He had a message for each of them as they navigated a life of faith in a world growing increasingly hostile against that faith. These letters are a worthwhile study, providing a framework for examining how we respond to our own cultural climate. Christ's message for these churches is as relevant for us as it was to them. In other words, these letters are evergreen.

Christians throughout the world today face various levels of hardship and persecution. Christian faith still gets tested by one storm after another. Culture pulls further away from God and questions our stubborn resistance to compromise. Headlines and social media feeds are filled with horrors of violence, abuse, corruption, and death, creating a quasi-autonomic response called "doom scrolling." How do we respond to all of this? How should

---

4   Revelation 1:3.

we respond? Should we jump into the various battles raging in culture? Which do we join? Which side do we take? How do we cultivate a faith in Jesus that is fresh, relevant, and functional while living in a culture propelling itself farther and farther from Him?

Believe it or not, the Revelation churches asked similar questions. Regardless of where or when, Christians will always live within a culture that rejects Christ and the gospel to varying degrees. These letters exhort believers—then and now—to closely analyze our responses to culture and make any necessary changes.

Blessed are those who read and those who hear and those who do the things which are written...for the time is near.

Blessing, not fear, is the reason Jesus gave His Revelation. Each letter ends with the same exhortation: "He who has an ear, let him hear what the Spirit says to the churches." There are truths that no amount of reading or writing can reveal, that are only learned when the Holy Spirit reveals them to us. We must incline our ears to hear what the Spirit is saying specifically to us through these letters. Hearing the voice of God can be difficult in a culture clamoring for our attention.[5] But, if we pause long enough to listen, we will hear Him saying, "This is the way, walk in it."[6] And as we heed His words, our faith will become more fervent, more steadfast.

Our faith will become evergreen.

---

[5]   I say "hearing" here, but I have never literally heard God's voice. At least, not in the way I see it in Scripture. Others may have, but I have not. Instead, my experience with the voice of the Lord is that I *feel* it. I may not literally hear Him, but I know beyond a shadow of a doubt that He has spoken to me.

[6]   Isaiah 30:21.

Chapter 1
Jesus is Near

The finished work of Revelation—including the letters—were originally meant to be sent to seven specific churches along the trade routes running through western Asia Minor.[1] The leaders of those churches would have read them aloud to their congregations, and the symbols and references in Revelation were more easily accessible to those audiences. Because we are separated by almost two millennia, it takes a little more work on our behalf to understand Christ's message to His people in this book. To help us in that endeavor, let's first examine the historical context surrounding the Revelation letters and the significance of John's vision of Jesus at that time.

Christians throughout the Roman empire faced tribulation, bias, and an "othering" that rendered them socially "less than." Domitian's revitalization of traditional Roman religion—including the imperial cult—forced believers into impossible situations. The cult promoted the divine nature of Domitian's rule, and Domitian himself took the title "Lord and God" while declaring his son a god and Domitia

---

1   Ephesus, Smyrna, Pergamum, Thyatira, Sardis, Philadelphia, and Laodicea.

(his mother) a goddess.[2] G.K. Beale notes that society viewed participation in the imperial cult as "expressions of loyalty" and "part of being patriotic," while refusal was "bad citizenship."[3] You weren't a "true Roman" unless you participated in the state religion and treated Domitian as divine. Dissenters became marked as atheists, a charge carrying penalties ranging from being banished from their hometown, to exile, or—on rare occasions—even execution.

It's hard to overstate the devastation of Domitian's rule for both Christians and Jews. Eusebius wrote, "Many were the victims of Domitian's appalling cruelty. At Rome great numbers of men distinguished by birth and attainments were for no reason at all banished from the country and their property confiscated."[4] Like Nero before him, Domitian ruled out of paranoia, and few were safe from his conspiracy-laden mind. He saw usurpers behind every stone and began executing "all who were of David's line," including the descendants of Jude, "the brother, humanly speaking, of the Saviour."[5] The specter of suspicion hung over the empire like thick smoke. Fear abounded and accusations flew, as many scrambled to find ways to keep the eye of the state off of themselves and their families. This included many in the Jewish community who sought to put distance between themselves and the new religious movement claiming Jesus as the only Lord, King, and Son of God. Fear and trauma put many in the empire into survival mode.

John, like so many other believers, faced these challenges courageously. Knowing the possible consequences, John refused to be silent on the matter of Jesus, and continued declaring Him as the Son of God and Savior of the world. For his efforts, John

2   Robert B. Hughes and J. Carl Laney, *Tyndale Concise Bible Commentary*, The Tyndale Reference Library (Wheaton, IL: Tyndale House Publishers, 2001), 727.
3   G.K. Beale, *The Book of Revelation: A Commentary on the Greek Text* (Grand Rapids, MI.: Wm. B. Eerdmans Publishing Co., 1999), 30.
4   Eusebius, *History of the Church*, trans. G.A. Williamson, (III.17), p. 80.
5   *ibid* (III.19), p. 81.

became a "fellow partaker in the tribulation and kingdom and perseverance which are in Jesus."[6] Domitian exiled him to the island of Patmos sometime around 93 CE. John's exile may have separated him from the community of believers, but it did not separate him from Christ Himself. In solitude and "in the spirit on the Lord's Day," John received a personal visit from Jesus Himself.[7]

Christ's visitation is reminiscent of similar moments recorded in the Old Testament: when Ezekiel saw "the heavens opened and visions of God" while exiled in Babylon[8]; when Shadrach, Meshack, and Abednego stood and talked with "one like the Son of God" while inside a fiery furnace[9]; when Moses saw a bush burning with the glory of God while shepherding alone in the wilderness.[10] God specializes in meeting us where we are. It's a reminder that there is no physical requirement to be in His presence: no building is necessary, no minimum number of participants, no elaborately crafted environment. All that is required is a willingness to be in the Spirit, to hit the proverbial pause button on our schedule and wait upon the Lord. Believers who do this find they are never really alone. Even when we feel isolated (John was literally exiled on an island), Jesus is nearer than we think.

Jesus's Position and Authority

While John suffered the punishment of the state, Jesus revealed Himself in the fullness of His glory. John describes Jesus with luminescent language: hair white like wool and snow, eyes like a flame of fire, and feet like burnished, glowing bronze. His visage is both awesome and terrible. Surely, Christ's authority far surpasses

---

6   Revelation 1:9.
7   Revelation 1:10.
8   Ezekiel 1:1.
9   Daniel 3:25, KJV.
10   Exodus 3:1-2.

that of Domitian and every other leader / dictator throughout the world's history. Jesus's power is incomparable. He alone is King, High Priest, and Son of God. His name is greater than all names. Christ is far above all powers and principalities yesterday, today, and forevermore.

John also describes Jesus as standing in the middle of seven golden lampstands and holding seven stars in His right hand. Revelation is full of figurative language where items, images, and events may be symbols with deeper meaning. The lampstands and stars are exactly that, and Jesus Himself gives the explanation:

> As for the mystery of the seven stars which you saw in My right hand, and the seven golden lampstands: the seven stars are the angels of the seven churches, and the seven lampstands are the seven churches.[11]

In John's vision, Jesus stands among the seven churches, holding their angels in His hand. Although John is exiled and Christians in the empire were suffering, John's vision ensured them (as it does us) that Jesus has not left or forsaken His people. Jesus, indeed, was near.

Christ Upholds His Church

The Greek word *angelos* (**ang**-el-os) translates as both "angel" and "messenger." The Old Testament book of Daniel may provide some insight to help us understand the use of stars here. While describing the coming judgment of the world, the angel of the Lord told Daniel, "Those who have insight will shine brightly like the brightness of the expanse of heaven, and those who lead the many to righteousness, like the stars forever and ever."[12] The stars, then, are the leaders of these seven churches, the people responsible for

---

11   Revelation 1:20.
12   Daniel 12:3.

spiritually nurturing the congregation. Jesus holds them in His right hand.

Jesus's own strength upholds the leaders of the seven churches. As we'll see in the following chapters, the Revelation churches existed in a tumultuous time when nothing remained established, nobody could be trusted, and even the ground itself seemed unsteady. The leaders of these churches had to navigate conflicting doctrines as well as protect themselves and their churches as best they could from those who sought their demise. Ministry was both dangerous and exhausting. Such conditions led some leaders to wrest control from the Lord, believing the notion that success in ministry depended on their ability, that their own grit and determination sustained the ministry of the church. Some leaders redefined what a successful ministry meant, adopting a world's view that is more easily seen and measured. Yet, Jesus holds the stars. His strength alone undergirds the angels of the churches. In fact, Paul indicated that Jesus's strength is perfected in our weaknesses.[13] We are not enough—we were never meant to be. Jesus, however, is more than enough.

It's OK to breathe. Jesus has you in His hands.

Ministry is daunting because the work is beyond the scope of a single lifetime and the stakes are eternal. There are days (months? years?) where accomplishing Jesus's mission to reach the world with the gospel seems impossible. This is a good thing. It reminds us of our desperate need for Him and His strength. Jesus is the vine; we are His branches. It reminds us that Christianity is not a solo act. We are a Church, connected to each other by the strength of Christ's love. We need each other. We need Jesus. It's a good thing, then, that He holds the stars and stands among the lampstands.

---

13   See 2 Corinthians 12:7-9.

While the image of Jesus holding the stars suggests His sustaining strength, the image of Him standing amidst the lampstands conveys His nearness. Practically speaking, the lampstands represented seven literal churches in Asia Minor to whom Revelation was sent. However, the number itself is also symbolic, gesturing toward the seven-day creation process recorded in Genesis. In that context, seven represents wholeness and completion. One commentary calls it, "the covenant number, the sign of God's covenant relation to mankind, and especially to the Church."[14] Seven lampstands, then, represent the entire Church, everywhere, at all times. This is why studying these letters is so important. Their value extends beyond those first-century churches, providing vital instruction for all believers who wrestle with responding to their own culture. The first lesson Jesus gives to Christians is contained in the symbol: we are lampstands in the world.

Golden lampstands gesture toward the lamp in the Jewish temple and indicate the function of the Church. The temple lamp was made of beaten gold and filled with oil as fuel for seven individual flames. Priests regularly replenished the oil, ensuring the Holy Place was continually bathed in light. Likewise, the Church emanates the light of Christ. Jesus taught His followers, "You are the light of the world."[15] Paul wrote, "You were formerly darkness, but now you are light in the Lord."[16] Christians are not the source of light. We are merely bearers of the true Light: Jesus. When we walk as children of Light, we radiate Christ's love in a dark world, and His light draws people to Himself.

---

14   Robert Jamieson, A.R. Fausset, and David Brown, *Commentary Critical and Explanatory on the Whole Bible* vol. 2 (Oak Harbor, WA: Logos Research Systems, Inc., 1997), 551.
15   Matthew 5:14.
16   Ephesians 5:8.

Lamps need fuel to burn. Old Testament priests daily replenished the oil in the temple lampstand, ensuring the flame never died. Like the priests of old, Jesus (our High Priest) tends to the oil fueling the flame in His Church. What is the oil? Great question!

The Church (as we know) is the lamp. The Holy Spirit is the oil. On the night of His betrayal, Jesus comforted His disciples, promising the Holy Spirit to them all, calling Him "another helper" that would "be with [them] forever."[17] For a church—indeed for any Christian—to continue bearing the light of Jesus in the world, we need to be continually refilled with the Holy Spirit. He empowers us for the mission given to us by Christ: preach the gospel, baptize believers, and make disciples. He provides the fuel necessary for us to let our light shine in such a way that people "glorify [our] Father who is in heaven." In the same way we find comfort in Jesus's sustaining strength, we find courage in the Holy Spirit's empowering strength.

How do we receive and become filled with the Holy Spirit? Simple: ask. Jesus compared parents with the Lord: "If you then, being evil, know how to give good gifts to your children, how much more will your heavenly Father give the Holy Spirit to those who ask Him?"[18] Those "gifts" that parents gave their children in Jesus's rhetorical question were daily needs. Jesus's not-so-subtle message: we need the Holy Spirit. However, we don't necessarily feel or acknowledge that need until we strive to be who Christ has called us to be, and do what He has called us to do in the world. We won't need the Comforter if our lives are comfortable.

When was the last time we asked the Lord to fill us with His presence, with the Holy Spirit? How evident in our lives are the

---

17 John 14:16.
18 Luke 11:13.

fruit of the Spirit: love, joy, peace, patience, kindness, goodness, faithfulness, gentleness, and self-control?[19] How dependent are we on the Holy Spirit's involvement in our lives? I'm reminded of Paul's first words to the handful of believers in Ephesus: "Have you received the Holy Ghost since you believed?"[20] It's easy to think of God as working in the abstract: He involves Himself in the activities of the Church. But His involvement is much more personal. He wants to fill you, individually, with His Spirit. All we have to do is acknowledge our need for Him and ask.

A lamp can shine without being refilled, but the oil will eventually run out. A lamp without light is just a decoration. If we deny the presence of the Lord in our lives, we run the risk of snuffing out the light shining in and through our lives. The oil runs out slowly, then all at once. We need the Holy Spirit in our churches and our personal lives. All we need to do is ask.

Christ Glorified

John titles his writing in the first line: "The Revelation of Jesus Christ." Christ's revelation begins almost immediately, with His visitation to John. Under the guidance of the Holy Spirit, John meticulously records every detail intentionally revealed to him. Grant Osborn argues that the details of John's vision of Christ do not require "separate and exact translation," but should be taken as a whole, evaluated for their "evocative and emotive power."[21] To be sure, John's vision of the glorified Christ is evocative. Shockingly so. However, the details John records are important. Indeed, Jesus refers to them in six of the seven letters. The imagery connects to Old Testament imagery and prophecy. Its historical and cultural

---

19   For more on the fruit of the Spirit, see Galatians 5:19-23.
20   Acts 19:2, KJV.
21   Grant R. Osborne, *Revelation*, Baker Exegetical Commentary on the New Testament (Grand Rapids, MI: Baker Academic, 2002), 89.

contexts are too significant to ignore. Nothing is more culturally relevant than clothing, and that's exactly where John begins his description.

In first-century Rome, clothing indicated a person's place in the social hierarchy. Commoners typically wore robes that reached their knees. Their shorter length increased mobility for daily labor. Osborn notes that laborers also wore sashes as belts across the waist so they could "tuck in a tunic for work."[22] Short robes and belts were the overalls and jeans of the Greco-Roman era. Men of high rank (kings, governors, etc.) wore long robes and sported sashes across their chests. John notes that Jesus's robe reached down to His feet, and He wore a golden sash across His chest. Both details identify Him as, "One with honor and authority."[23] To be sure, Jesus is the King of Kings and Lord of Lords. He is also our High Priest. Jewish historian, Josephus indicates that a priests' vestment included a sash "with a mixture of gold interwoven" as well as robes that "reach down to the feet, and sits close to the body."[24] Jesus reveals Himself to John as both King and Priest, dignified and highly exalted above all else.

John describes the head and hair of Jesus as both wool and snow. I believe the Holy Spirit impressed these two unrelated similes upon John when describing the color (and texture) of Jesus's hair. Throughout the Bible, authors use white to describe something pure or flawless. Figuratively, white symbolizes holiness. Snow is naturally white. It's why we have the phrase "pure as the driven snow" to describe a person's innocence or virtue. Describing Jesus's white hair as being like snow suggests holiness is part of Jesus's

22   *Ibid.*
23   Warren W. Wiersbe, *The Bible Exposition Commentary*, vol. 2 (Wheaton, IL: Victor Books, 1996), 569.
24   Josephus, *The Works of Josephus: Complete and Unabridged*, trans. William Whiston, (Peabody, MA: Hendrickson Publishers, Inc., 2004), 88-89.

nature. Christ is holy. Wool, however, requires an arduous process of scouring to become white. Woolen fibers are soaked and beaten to drive out oils and dirt. Wool, then, suggests Jesus's humanity. As a man, Jesus was tempted the same ways we are, but He never sinned.[25] Jesus is holy. He is the Son of God and the Son of Man.

Jesus's white hair also indicates His eternality. Over five centuries earlier, Daniel had a vision with details very much like John's:

> I kept looking until thrones were set up, and the Ancient of Days took His seat; His vesture was like white snow and the hair of His head like pure wool. His throne was ablaze with flames, its wheels were a burning fire.[26]

Daniel received his vision while exiled in Babylon. John received his while exiled on Patmos. In Daniel's vision, one like a son of man approached the Ancient of Days. In John's vision, Jesus—the Son of Man and Son of God—*is* the Ancient of Days. In both visions, God showed Himself as established before the beginning of time. The Ancient of Days exists from eternal past into eternal future. He ruled long before the establishment of kingdoms, empires, and dominions; and He will exist long after they are forgotten. Jesus is the same yesterday, today, and forever. His wisdom demands our highest respect and attention. It ought to be carefully sought after and considered. He is Ancient of Days, and His judgment will be sound, just, and true.

One of the more evocative elements of John's vison are Jesus's eyes, which blaze like a flame of fire. Again, John and Daniel's experiences bear remarkable similarities, as Daniel describes the man who visited him as having "eyes like flaming torches."[27] Eyes

---

25   See Hebrews 4:15.
26   Daniel 7:9.
27   Daniel 10:6.

of fire indicate a penetrating gaze that not only sees our actions but the motives behind them. We tend to live behind masks, presenting highly-curated images of ourselves in public. His eyes see beyond our masks, filters, walls, and the myriad other ways we lie to ourselves and others. Jesus sees exactly who we are. His eyes are like a flame of fire.

Fire strongly suggests Jesus's intention for looking at us, particularly as He stands amid the lampstands. Malachi asks of the coming Messiah, "Who can endure the day of His coming? For He is like a refiner's fire."[28] A refiner's fire heats metal to a point where all impurities (dross) rise to the surface, allowing the refiner to remove them. Fire consumes, and there is no hiding from Jesus's gaze. Jesus constantly works in, through, and among His people. His goal isn't to condemn us for being impure, but to reveal our impurities so they can be removed. By grace we are saved through faith; and by grace we are changed from glory to glory into the image of Jesus.

John describes Jesus's feet as bronze glowing in fire. Fire and bronze gesture toward the functional elements of the temple courtyard. A bronze tub called a "laver" sat directly in front of the entrance into the Holy Place of the temple. Crafted from highly-polished bronze, the laver reflected a priest's humanity back to him while he washed his hands and feet, ceremonially purifying himself in preparation for the work before the Holy One inside. A bronze altar dominated the tableau of the temple courtyard. Fire burned within it throughout the day, consuming sacrifices made by priests for themselves and for the people of Israel. Fire and bronze, then, symbolize judgment and purification of God's people. Jesus wears them on His feet, suggesting mobility. Jesus brings perfect judgment in order to purify His people. His pronouncements are

---

28   Malachi 3:2.

meant to further sanctify His people, strengthening their faith to withstand the winds of cultural change.

John's vision includes the auditory description of Jesus's voice as "the sound of many waters."[29] Throughout His ministry, Jesus synthesized the many voices of the Law and prophets into the command to love God with everything you have and to love others as yourself. He considered these the greatest commandments.[30] That simple message challenged all who heard it. It still does. Some accepted His "new commandment," while others rejected both it and Him as heretical. People still do. One day, every one of us will realize that His Word has been true all along. Until then, Jesus's Word continues to convict and challenge us to live more like Him.

I often wonder what (if anything) John saw coming from Jesus's mouth. Certainly, it could not have been a literal two-edged sword. He seems to be referencing the Messianic message in Isaiah: "[The Lord] has made My mouth like a sharp sword."[31] The Hebrews author did the same, describing Scripture as a sharp two-edged sword, adding that the Word of God can perfectly "judge the thoughts and intentions of the heart."[32] A two-edged sword cuts both ways. It is efficient and effective for penetrating and cutting. Describing Jesus's Word as a two-edged sword indicates the power and purpose of His message. Like His eyes, Jesus's word cuts through our façades and our masks, revealing the truth of who we are. Some things in our lives and some aspects of our character need to be removed. God's Word does just that. It may overwhelm us like the roar of rushing waters, but His truth also carries the potential to transform us if we listen and act upon it.

---

29   Revelation 1:15.
30   See Matthew 22:36-40.
31   Isaiah 49:2
32   Hebrews 4:12

John's Response (and Ours)

Reading John's vision of Jesus is a relatively simple thing, especially in a chapter evaluating the details of what John saw. However, by examining the proverbial trees, we tend to lose the awe-inspiring grandeur of the forest. John buckled under his vision of Jesus. "I fell at His feet like a dead man," he wrote. Who wouldn't? Nobody had seen Jesus like this. Commentator Warren Wiersbe writes, "This vision of Christ was totally different in appearance from the Saviour that John knew…He was not the 'gentle Jewish carpenter' that sentimentalists like to sing about. He is the risen, glorified, exalted Son of God, the Priest-King who has the authority to judge all men, beginning with His own people."[33] John's response is the normal, expected response of anyone who finds themselves face to face with Christ glorified. It is also the normal, expected response of anyone who fully realizes their own sinfulness in the context of God's holiness—when we understand that our sin eternally separates us from a holy God; that eternal punishment is our just reward; and that nothing we do erases our sinful nature. In short, we fall down as dead when confronted with God's perfect holiness. This response is right and proper, indicating a godly sorrow that leads to repentance.[34]

What happens next is extraordinary.

Rather than bask in John's fearful obeisance, Jesus comforts him with the words, "Do not be afraid."[35] John records that Jesus also placed His right hand on him in consolation. Picture it. Jesus, in all His glory, reached down and touched John to relieve his discomfort. As readers, it feels almost voyeuristic as we spy a tender moment

---

33   Warren W. Wiersbe, *The Bible Exposition Commentary*, 569.
34   See 2 Corinthians 7:10-11.
35   The King James renders this phrase as "Fear not." It's a slightly more forceful statement but produces the same comfort in John (and his readers).

shared between John and His Lord, a moment where we see the loving hand of the Good Shepherd comforting one of His sheep. Jesus placed His right hand, the hand of strength, on John. John's strength failed when he saw Christ glorified. Jesus gave him all the strength he needed through a touch and a word. But it's even more incredible than that. John had fallen as a dead man: flat on the ground. To reach him, Jesus would have had to kneel.

Jesus knelt.

We have no more perfect image for salvation than the glorified Jesus kneeling before John, comforting him. John did not fall at Jesus's feet as a poor man or an uneducated man. Neither sickness nor injury caused John to collapse. John fell at Jesus's feet as a dead man. And Jesus knelt. "The wages of sin is death," Paul wrote, "but the free gift of God is eternal life in Christ Jesus our Lord."[36] The image of Christ kneeling before John powerfully illustrates that free gift given through the condescension of the Lord. Our sinful choices have put us on the path of death and destruction. But Jesus still kneels to comfort those who fall at His feet as dead.

Because of Jesus, we can walk with confidence. Not because we are special, or gifted, or well-suited, but because we follow the Victorious One. He is our High Priest, the King of Kings, the Son of God, our Savior, and our friend. "You are my friends," Jesus told His disciples, "if you do what I command you."[37] Who but the Son of God could say such a thing?

Do not be afraid. What a beautiful message after experiencing Jesus in all His terrifying, awe-inspiring majesty.

Do not be afraid. What a powerful consolation to a people enduring persecution, facing social exile, violence, even death.

36   Romans 6:23.
37   John 15:14.

Do not be afraid. Jesus's comforting word to John still echoes as powerfully in the twenty-first century as it did in the first. Heaven and earth will pass away, but His Word will never pass away.

Although the person standing before John terrified him, Jesus was there to help His people, not destroy them; to comfort them, not condemn them. The same is true today. Jesus stands among His Church, healing and comforting and convicting and teaching and challenging His people to remain steadfast in an ever-changing world. He never instructed His followers to live in a protective bubble, but to live in the world among the worldly, being salt and light, and drawing all people to Him. Jesus knows how influential His people can be in the world. He also knows how influential the world can be on His people. In John's vision, in the seven letters, and through the entire book of Revelation, Jesus stands with His people, giving them comfort, correction, and (if needed) judgment.

John's vision of Jesus sets Him apart from everyone else on the planet, throughout history. Christians in John's day lived in fear of Domitian's decrees against them. But One far greater than Domitian stood with them. His authority, His power, indeed His name is above every other name. There has never been—nor will there ever be—a ruler or empire that compares to Christ. Because of Jesus's authority, His deity, and His glory, we cannot question or ignore His judgment. Because of His holiness, eternality, and clear-sightedness, we don't need to fear His judgment. Instead, we should seek His gaze and embrace His judgment, because if anyone can judge us properly (indeed, perfectly), it is Jesus. Who better than the One whose character and expectations have never changed through the millennia? Holiness is Christ's nature, and He will never change. His judgment will always be true, and we can trust His Word at all times.

God promised that He would never leave nor forsake His people. Moses tended a flock in the wilderness, but he wasn't alone. Jonah found himself isolated in the belly of a fish, but he wasn't alone. God was with both of them. Likewise, Jesus promised that He would be with His disciples "even to the end of the age."[38] John was exiled on a tiny Greek island, but he was not alone. Jesus was there. His disciples will always face daunting circumstances in a world at odds with the Lord. However, Jesus's assured proximity grants the ability to endure any and all hardships confidently.

Can you imagine how those congregations might have responded to this vision of Jesus? He is radiating power and standing in the middle of the churches. What would that have meant to those enduring persecution? How might it have encouraged those whose very lives were being threatened by their neighbors and the government under which they lived? Can you see them all holding their breath as John's vision is described? Can you hear them release that breath when hearing Jesus say, "Do not be afraid"? Can you see them all subconsciously leaning in as the orator reads, "Now unto the angel of the church in Ephesus write…"

Wherever and whenever believers live, they face tough, unsettling times. Jesus, the beginning and the end, is our Rock, our immovable, unshifting ground. What sort of circumstances are you facing today? What hardships are you enduring? Do you feel isolated and alone in your struggles? It may feel more convenient to use our circumstances as an excuse to ignore—or even avoid—the presence of the Lord. John chose to seek Him out on Patmos, to be in the Spirit on the Lord's Day; and he found (like you and I will find) that he was not alone. Jesus was right there with him.

---

38   Matthew 28:20.

Dear friend, if you are facing an obstacle that seems insurmountable; if you are facing a battle that seems unwinnable; if you are facing a problem that seems unsolvable, never forget: Jesus is near.

Revelation 2:1–7

1 *"To the angel of the church in Ephesus write: The One who holds the seven stars in His right hand, the One who walks among the seven golden lampstands, says this:*

2 *'I know your deeds and your toil and perseverance, and that you cannot tolerate evil men, and you put to the test those who call themselves apostles, and they are not, and you found them to be false;*

3 *and you have perseverance and have endured for My name's sake, and have not grown weary.*

4 *'But I have this against you, that you have left your first love.*

5 *'Therefore remember from where you have fallen, and repent and do the deeds you did at first; or else I am coming to you and will remove your lampstand out of its place—unless you repent.*

6 *'Yet this you do have, that you hate the deeds of the Nicolaitans, which I also hate.*

7 *'He who has an ear, let him hear what the Spirit says to the churches. To him who overcomes, I will grant to eat of the tree of life which is in the Paradise of God.'*

Chapter 2
The Letter to Ephesus

Situated on the western coast of Asia Minor, Ephesus (near modern-day Selçuk) was the first of seven cities Jesus addressed along the trade routes extending eastward. Ephesus itself was an economic powerhouse. With a port and three main land routes running through it, the city was a major trading hub connecting Asia Minor with the rest of the Mediterranean. Like all port cities, Ephesus enjoyed a rich ethnic and cultural diversity. News and ideas came through the city like commodities. Life in the city revolved around three main activities: trade, religion, and imperialism: Ephesians traded many goods and worshiped many gods, all for the glory of Rome. Within this complex cultural mosaic stood a small, yet zealous, group of followers of a new religion called "The Way."[1]

Much of the cultural and economic identity of Ephesus was wrapped up in the worship of the Greek goddess Artemis (Roman: Diana) and the imperial cult. People from all over the world came to Ephesus to visit or worship at the Temple of Artemis, one of the seven wonders of the ancient world. Craftsmen greatly profited from selling icons and statues. Anything posing a threat to profits

---

1   See Acts 9:2, Acts 19:9 & 23, and Acts 24:14 & 22.

needed to be expelled. So, when Christianity made its way through Ephesus and local interest in Artemis receded, artisans—specifically silversmiths specializing in statues and shrines—instigated violence toward Christians.[2]

In the late first century, Ephesus became a *Neokoros*, or temple warden city, housing the newly built temple to Domitian. The title was both highly esteemed and sought after among the cities of the eastern Roman empire. As a *Neokoros*, the practice of worshiping Domitian and his family became more than another pagan celebration—it was an expression of patriotism and devotion to the empire. Citizens viewed non-participation as disloyal to the city and to Rome, which put Christians in constant danger of becoming social pariahs because of their faith in Christ.

But pressure didn't come only come from outside of Christianity. Jesus mentions the Nicolaitans by name to the Ephesian and Pergamos churches. According to Ireneus, Nicolaitans were followers of a man named Nicolas, "who was one of the seven first ordained to the diaconate by the apostles."[3] He is referring to the sixth chapter of Acts, when Nicolas was one seven men chosen to serve the widows of Hellenistic Jews in Jerusalem. Nicolas remained faithful in his lifetime. His followers, however, warped the Christian mandate of following Jesus on His terms. They not only adopted compromise, but made leading "lives of unrestrained indulgence" a part of their doctrine.[4] Nicolaitans, then, considered themselves Christians, but lived far from what anyone would define as Christ-like. In a world demanding compromise, Nicolaitan doctrine seemed to offer the perfect solution.

2　　See Acts 19. The entire chapter is a good primer for the religious context of Ephesus.

3　　Ireneus, *Against Heresies*, trans. Alexander Roberts, (I.26.3).

4　　*ibid.*

Paul's letter to the Ephesians suggests the church had been struggling early on with false teachers. They wrestled with how to consistently "speak the truth in love" in a culture that vacillates between indifference and hostility.[5] They struggled with the cultural insistence on compromise, especially when their lives and livelihood were on the line. The Revelation letter provided some direction for them. Christ's message doesn't address all their concerns, but He speaks directly about their experiences, giving them a framework from which to respond to—and live within—their culture.

Jesus's Position and Authority

It is generally agreed that Jesus addressed these letters to the leaders of the churches, who would then read them to the congregations. The Youngs Literal Translation, for example, renders the introduction for each letter as, "To the messenger of the assembly at…" Jesus's greeting, then, signifies the level of accountability each of those leaders carried and to Whom they were accountable. It also suggests that, as leaders, they heavily influenced a church's response to their cultural environment.

Church leaders are different from business leaders. In the Old and New Testaments, the term "pastor" is used to describe leaders. The word literally means "shepherd" and describes two relationships: the one between the leader and their followers, and the one between the leader and Christ Himself. Jesus is the Good Shepherd, and the Church is His flock. Church leaders are not chief executives; they are under-shepherds responsible for a small portion of Jesus's flock. Jesus used pastoral language with Peter, telling him three times to tend to His sheep.[6] Leaders are answerable to Christ for how they tend His sheep—how they protect them, feed them, and

---

5   Ephesians 4:14-19.
6   John 21:15-17

nurture them. Jesus intensely watches how church leaders use the position and influence He has given to them.

In the context of responding to our culture, perhaps the most important thing to remember is Whose we are. Christ introduces Himself to Ephesus as the One who holds the seven stars and who stands amid the lampstands. In the previous chapter, we learned the lampstands represent the churches, and the stars signify the angels or leaders of those churches. Perhaps Ephesus forgot that Jesus holds them, that He is their strength. Fear can do that. Fear makes us lose sight of Jesus's position and authority, that He alone is the source of authority, of giftedness, of ministry, and of salvation. Jesus is the sustaining strength of His Church, the Good Shepherd of His flock. Jesus is the only One standing amid the lampstands, and He alone holds the seven stars.

One typical response to fear is an almost compulsive need for control. This was the problem in Ephesus. As we'll see in the next section, the church constructed a process for ensuring nothing false could ever enter the doors of the church—no false doctrine, no false teachers, no false Christians. They had created a literal test for people to pass in order to be accepted into their fellowship. The illusion of control convinces us that our efforts produce results, that righteousness is a product of self-will, that the gospel is our message, and we are responsible for other people's salvation. These are simply burdens we were never meant to carry, and the weight of them eventually crushes the joy of our own salvation. As Christians, we're meant to intentionally pursue Christ and people with love in faith. All the while, trusting Jesus alone for any results.

From His vantage point amid the lampstands (churches), Jesus sees everything. To the Ephesians, Jesus said, "I know your deeds and your toil and perseverance." The word translated "toil" comes from the Greek *kopos* (**kop**-os), which carries the implication of intense labor resulting in weariness. Barclay described it as "the kind of toil which takes everything of mind and sinew that a man can put into it."[7] Life in Ephesus was not easy for believers, yet the church persevered; and Jesus commended their endurance. Their energetic defense of the gospel never waned. Their love for the gospel itself, however, was a different story.

They Left their First Love

Some of the deeds Jesus notes are the Ephesians' intolerance of evil men and their testing of people claiming apostleship, a title marking a person as an eminent teacher. On their own, these are not bad. John wrote a letter in which he said, "Beloved, do not believe every spirit, but test the Spirits to see whether they are from God."[8] Paul warned the Corinthian church of men who were "false apostles, deceitful workers, disguising themselves as apostles of Christ."[9] The church at Ephesus, under the guidance of the angel of the church, did all they could to ensure no false doctrine could enter the church. Yet, the language Jesus used ("you cannot tolerate" and "you put to the test") suggests something is amiss in the hearts of His people at Ephesus. His criticism cuts to their core: "You have left your first love."

What, exactly, did Jesus mean by "first love"? What is our first love; and how can we leave it? Jesus's council later in the letter (which we examine in the next section) helps us understand: "repent and do the deeds you did at first." It seems whatever changed in the hearts of the believers happened somewhere between when they first believed and when Jesus sends this letter. Understanding

---

7   William Barclay, *The Revelation of John* vol. 1 (Louisville KY: Westminster John Knox Press, 1976), 62.

8   1 John 4:1.

9   1 Corinthians 11:13.

our first love, then, requires us to remember what we felt when we first believed.

I'm sure we've all heard countless stories of people coming to Jesus. We've heard men, women, and children recounting powerful memories of receiving forgiveness, salvation, and hope from the Son of God. As diverse as those testimonies are, each contain a common denominator: a love for Jesus dominates each one. Sin gets exchanged with the love of God and a love for God, and what follows is an unbridled excitement about Christ and the things of God. Our hearts fill with an effervescent spring of emotion. We don't know Him well, but we want to. We don't know exactly how to serve Him, but we want to. Our lives take on new shape, with Christ at the center. Jesus becomes our number one pursuit. Everything else pales in comparison.

Jesus Himself is our first love.

In searching out heresy, the Ephesians lost sight of Christ. Their toil had taken a toll. Withstanding the constant barrage of pagan practices and false teaching wore them down, hardening their hearts. Speaking of the last days, Jesus warns that because of sin "most people's love will grow cold."[10] Who would have guessed that would include Jesus's own followers?

That is not to say Jesus is against doctrine being taught in the church, or against a church or Christians protecting themselves against false teaching. However, the Ephesian church was out of balance. John writes that Jesus came into the world "full of grace and truth."[11] Wherever He went, Jesus interacted with pagans, prostitutes, corrupt officials, and every other type of sinner. Regardless of who He was with, however, He spoke truth in a

---

10   Matthew 24:12.
11   John 1:14.

way that touched every hearer. Not everyone agreed with Jesus (some wanted to kill Him), but everyone understood the truth and felt the invitation to grace. Jesus never pandered to a crowd or minimized the seriousness of sin. He preached truth in love with grace and gentleness. His is the sort of balance each of us should consider in our interactions with others.

As followers of Jesus, we must take great pains to not treat grace and truth as opposing points on a gradient, diametrically opposed to one another. In an article for *Christianity Today*, Ronni Kurtz writes about the growing animosity in American churches, church leaders, and Christians in general based on differing points of belief and religious practice.

> Points of doctrine become the boundary lines in which an "us versus them" war plays out. And while there are indeed good and right times to draw lines in the sand, there are also those whose theological boundaries are so ever-shrinking that only they and a handful of their followers are seen as those who possess the truth.[12]

Winning arguments is the wrong goal for right theology. I'll put it another way: if convincing others is the primary purpose of our theology, we (and our churches) are on the same road as Ephesus. We may think we're on the righteous path, but in reality, we are on the path that takes us further from Christ, our first love. The goal of theology is knowing God. The goal of doctrine is preaching the gospel with our words and deeds. That's it.

Jesus's indictment against the Ephesian church is startling. *You have left your first love.* How does that happen? "Left" suggests agency. No church intends to leave Jesus, but that's exactly what happened. Andy Stanley identifies what he calls the Principle of the

---

12   Ronni Kurtz, "Why Are There So Many Angry Theologians?", *Christianity Today*, Jan. 3, 2023. https://www.christianitytoday.com/ct/2023/januaryfebruary/book-awards-kurtz-fruitful-theology-angry-theologians.html. Accessed online 8 Jan 2023.

Path, that "direction—not intention—determines our destination."[13] Amazing alliteration aside, the principle is solid. How many times have we intended for one thing to happen, only to have something entirely different come to pass? Every couple at the wedding altar intends for their marriage to last "until death do us part." However, many couples make decisions that set them on a direction leading toward marital disaster. It was their direction, not their intention, that determined the destination of their relationship. In the same way, nobody gives their lives to Jesus intending to leave Him some day. Leaving Jesus is never one decision. Instead, it's a series of small, subtle decisions that seem meaningless at the time, but add up to disaster. The church in Ephesus did not accidentally lose Christ, they left Him; and they probably had no idea until this letter arrived. Leaving Jesus was never their intention, but it became their reality.

The Ephesians were still a church doing all the "church" things, but they had left their first love. Jesus's rebuke reminds us that it is possible to perform religious activity and community service yet have no love for Christ or others. We can get so caught up in culture or heresy wars that we make duty, or obligation, or even moral superiority, our motive for serving in the Kingdom of God. The Ephesians may have loved Jesus, but Christ Himself suggests their activity came from a place of obligation rather than love. One commentator puts it succinctly: "Their warmth of love had given place to a lifeless orthodoxy."[14] Their enthusiasm may have begun from a place of love, but it had become rote: mindless and heartless routine. Indeed, Christianity was no longer a labor of love. It was just labor.

In his letter to the Corinthians, Paul explains the importance of love in the life of believers. He notes that love gives meaning to

---

13   Andy Stanley, *The Principle of the Path* (Nashville, Tn: Thomas Nelson, 2008), 14.
14   Jamieson, et al, *Commentary Critical and Explanatory on the Whole Bible*, 555.

our words, substance to our actions, and value to our sacrifices. His conclusion to this argument is chilling: we are nothing without love and even our most sacrificial service profits us nothing if it is not done in love.[15] Paul's argument implies that Christians can be blind to a faith that is lifeless and loveless, that we can dutifully serve the Kingdom, but have a hardened heart. Jesus taught that His disciples will be marked by love: "By this all men will know that you are My disciples, *if you have love for one another.*"[16] A loveless church is not a church of Jesus's disciples. If believers do not love people, how can they expect to effectively preach the gospel and lead people to Jesus? Christ's letter to the Ephesians is a call to return to our first love. When a love for Christ dominates our hearts and minds, a love for people is sure to follow.

Remember, Repent, and Return

A life of faith is guided by the love of Jesus. To continue in that faith and love, we need Christ to constantly search our hearts. "Test yourselves," Paul wrote to the Corinthian church, "to see if you are in the faith; examine yourselves!"[17] The Ephesians focused their tests on others when they should have been equally concerned with testing themselves, and Jesus called them out on it.

The Revelation letters present the pattern of God's work in us: He convicts, and we respond. Conviction is pointing out areas in our life where we are wrong, or where our attitudes are not aligned with God's character. We typically feel conviction through the emotion of guilt, an emotion we tend to avoid. However, when the Lord convicts, it is the first step toward transformation—something every disciple of Jesus desires. Godly sorrow sometimes comes through

---

15   1 Corinthians 13:1-3.
16   John 13:35, emphasis mine.
17   2 Corinthians 13:5

unexpected avenues. I've been convicted by God while praying, while preaching, while reading the Bible, while shopping, while driving—you get the picture. The Holy Spirit is good at interrupting our well-known routines, revealing any disparity between His will and our reality. Once that happens, we are presented with two options: agree with Him and repent, or disagree and rebel.

The Ephesians turned Christianity into religious duty, so Jesus sent a message of conviction: "You have left your first love." What's beautiful is that His message doesn't end there. Jesus never drops a conviction without also giving His counsel for correction. Jesus directs the Ephesian church (and anyone who has left their first love) to remember from where they had fallen and repent. "Fallen" is a word that implies loss—loss of status, position, or influence. A loveless approach to their community endangered the church's ability to reach that community with the love of God. Their church culture struck no balance between grace and truth, so they were losing an already tenuous standing with the community. They had fallen—not all at once, mind you, but little by little, intentionally yet incrementally moving further and further from the love of Jesus. Had He not sent them this letter, they may never have known their fallen state. It is vital for us to allow Jesus to examine our hearts, and convict us with what He sees.

Remember from where you have fallen, and repent. Growth and movement in the right direction only happens when energy is intentionally and consistently applied. His call to remember is a call to pause our busy activity and direct our energy toward reflecting on the path already traveled with the Lord. Remember the moment He forgave our sin and washed us from all unrighteousness. Remember the grace and love of God displayed on the cross, and the gratefulness we had when we first realized the implications of His sacrifice. Remember the excitement we once had for knowing

Jesus and making Him known. Remember the hunger we had for the things of God and for the Word of God. When David sinned against God (and against Bathsheba and her husband), he prayed, "Restore to me the joy of Your salvation."[18] Oh Lord, help us remember from where we have fallen!

Jesus's full counsel to Ephesus is to remember and repent. Repentance is not simply intellectual assent or emotional response. That's conviction, and conviction is merely the catalyst for repentance. Repentance actually begins when we change our minds and attitudes toward whatever the Lord has revealed. It continues as we pray, asking for forgiveness and guidance. Repentance finds fulfillment as we then commit ourselves to changing our ways, living more in line with God's definition of holiness and righteousness. As disciples of Jesus, our aim is to be more like Him. Repentance is the engine of that transformation. Repentance is not just a prayer. Repentance is a lifestyle.

For Ephesus, repentance began with remembering from where they had fallen. It continued with doing "the deeds you did at the first."[19] What were the things Ephesus did when they first came to the Lord? Nobody knows exactly, but Acts 19 gives us some hints:

- Believers were baptized in the name of the Lord Jesus (vs. 5).
- God performed "extraordinary miracles by the hands of Paul" (vs. 11).
- Fear of the Lord fell on the city; the name of Jesus was magnified; many confessed their sin; and many more destroyed the pagan idols and books in their possession. (vss. 17-19).

Luke's narrative in that chapter clearly illustrates a fervent devotion and love for Christ. In response, God performed miracles, confirming the gospel being preached, and many people far from God came to know Jesus through the church's ministry.

---

18   Psalms 51:12. For more on David's sin, read 2 Samuel 11 & 12.
19   Revelation 2:5.

A lot changed between then and this letter. Christ's direction to do their first deeds suggests they had stopped doing them. They were no longer reaching into the community with the gospel. Instead, they became religious gatekeepers, standing guard against heresy. That seems fine on the surface, but in a city full of heretics, who is allowed into church gatherings? This letter suggests that the church had turned inward, putting up walls of protection. Rather than reaching the lost like we see in Acts 19, the Ephesian church shut them out. What a fall!

Jesus ends this portion of His letter with a chilling warning: if they didn't repent, He would "remove [their] lampstand out of its place." The lampstand represented the church itself. Jesus warns that if they don't fundamentally change—repent—He would remove them from among the Church. In the words of George Beasley-Murray: "The removal of the lampstand from its place can signify nothing less than the end of Christ's recognition of the church as a church of his. It will become as devoid of Christ as the temple of Jerusalem became empty of God prior to its destruction."[20] A harsh but just response. A church without love may be a church, but it's not a church of Jesus's disciples.

While it's important to guard against false doctrine, it's equally important to maintain our love for God and for people—all people. That is sometimes easier said than done. Ephesus shows us how hard it is to maintain a life of love and faith in an increasingly antagonistic culture. But the stakes are too high not to. We must resist the temptation to do the right thing for the wrong reasons, resist the magnetic pull from being a loving disciple of Christ to simply a religious person dutifully performing the expected activities.

---

20   George R. Beasley-Murray, "Revelation." *New Bible Commentary: 21st Century Edition.* Ed. D. A. Carson et al. 4th ed. Leicester, England; Downers Grove, IL: Inter-Varsity Press, 1994. 1428. Print.

Jesus will always be in the midst of the lampstands, but *we* won't remain unless we remember, repent, and return to Him.

Eden Restored

Another common element in all the Revelation letters is a promise to all who overcome. To Ephesus, Jesus promises to grant overcomers the ability to "eat of the tree of life which is in the Paradise of God." This is more than a return to the Garden of Eden—it is entry into that which the garden foreshadowed.

The creation narrative in Genesis describes the Lord planting a garden in Eden as a dwelling place for newly-created man. J. Daniel Hays writes, "God does not create the garden of Eden merely to give Adam and Even a nice place to live, but He creates it as a special place where they can have a relationship with Him and live a wonderful life blessed by His presence."[21] The garden was God's first temple, and for an undisclosed amount of time, Adam, Eve, and the Lord enjoyed close fellowship. Genesis casually mentions the Lord "walking in the garden in the cool of the day."[22] Eventually, creation rebelled against their creator, eating from the tree of knowledge of good and evil, severing the relationship between themselves and the God Who made them. The Lord's response was severe, expelling Adam and Eve from the garden and forever cutting them off from the tree of life.[23]

Overcomers enjoy small tastes of Eden in this life. Through Christ, the broken relationship between mankind and the Lord is restored. Jesus purchased our redemption through His death,

---

21   J. Daniel Hays, *The Temple and the Tabernacle: A study of God's dwelling places from Genesis to Revelation*, (Grand Rapids, MI: Baker Books, 2016), p. 21.
22   Genesis 3:8.
23   Even this, however, was grace since God had told them from the outset, "In the day you eat [from the tree of knowledge of good and evil] you will die."

taking our sins (our rebellion) upon Himself, dying in our place, and paying our debt to the Lord. Because of His great act of love, "all who call upon the name of the Lord shall be saved." We can experience a vibrant, thriving relationship with the Lord similar to the one enjoyed by Adam and Eve in the garden.

Additionally, Jesus promises access to the tree of life, which now stands in the Paradise of God. The word "paradise" originated with the Persians, who used it to describe a grand enclosure or preserve or a shady, well-watered park in which wild animals were kept. It evokes a verdant image, full of foliage and teeming with life. G.K. Beale astutely argues that "the image of the 'tree of life' together with the 'Paradise of God' symbolizes the life-giving presence of God, from which Adam and Eve are separated when they are cast out of the garden paradise."[24] What Jesus promises here, then, is nothing less than the return of paradise in its fullest sense.

What Christians enjoy in part now, they will enjoy in full later. But we need to overcome, endure, persevere. Jesus never promised that following Him would be easy. He often indicated it would be difficult, nearly impossible. But He did promise that He would always be with us; that the Holy Spirit would strengthen us and empower us; that our Father in heaven would look on us and see Jesus in us. All of our experiences and encounters with the Lord today are but a foretaste of what is to come. It reminds me of the old hymn, "Blessed Assurance":

> *Blessed assurance, Jesus is mine;*
> *Oh, what a foretaste of glory divine!*
> *Heir of salvation, purchase of God,*
> *Born of His Spirit, washed in His blood.*[25]

---

24   Beale, *The Book of Revelation*, 235.
25   Fanny Jane Crosby, "Blessed Assurance," 1873.

Dear friend, don't give up. No matter how angry the world gets around you, respond with love. Keep loving people and loving Jesus well. It's not easy. The constant cultural onslaught against Christianity wore the Ephesians down to mere hard-hearted shadows of their former selves. The importance of the work of protecting a church against spiritual predators and false doctrine cannot be overstated. However, heresy-hunting and doctrinal tests must never replace the joy of our salvation, a joy Peter describes as "inexpressible and full of glory."[26] Jesus is our joy. Amidst all the work of ministry we shoulder, regardless of the push-back we get from friends, family, and society at large, in spite of a culture that rewards independence, the absolute vital thing for all of us is to maintain a close, vibrant, intimate relationship with the Lord.

If your love has run cold, remember from where you've fallen, repent, and return to those first works. Return to your first love. He's never left. Jesus is our strength, our shield, and our true reward. And—like the Ephesians—He is calling you back to Himself.

---

26   1 Peter 1:8.

Revelation 2:8–11

8 *"And to the angel of the church in Smyrna write: The first and the last, who was dead, and has come to life, says this:*

9 *'I know your tribulation and your poverty (but you are rich), and the blasphemy by those who say they are Jews and are not, but are a synagogue of Satan.*

10 *'Do not fear what you are about to suffer. Behold, the devil is about to cast some of you into prison, so that you will be tested, and you will have tribulation for ten days. Be faithful until death, and I will give you the crown of life.*

11 *'He who has an ear, let him hear what the Spirit says to the churches. He who overcomes will not be hurt by the second death.'*

Chapter 3
The Letter to Smyrna

The first-century city of Smyrna already had a wealth of history in its wake by the time John's letter reached them. Some historians believe it was founded around 3000 BCE, rising to prominence during the Iron Age. Its location at the mouth of the Hermus river with a port to the Aegean Sea made Smyrna a thriving city of trade, rich in cultural diversity and political clout.

Like Ephesus, Smyrna was a *Neokoros*, a temple-warden city. It was also one of the first cities to recognize Rome as a rising empire. Seeking to align itself against the surrounding Seleucid Dynasty, Smyrna enthusiastically built a temple to the goddess Rome (Greek *Rômê*, meaning "power") some time before 195 BCE.[1] This marked the early beginnings of the Roman imperial cult, which recognized emperors as divine and worthy of worship, complete with temples built in their name. Because of Smyrna's stalwart support, the imperial senate awarded the city with the title *Neokoros* in 26 CE, allowing it to build a temple honoring Caesar Tiberius. The title granted the city rights to organize festivals, drawing enormous crowds of pilgrims

---

[1]   Murat Kiliç. "The Roman Imperial Cult in Smyrna." *Belleten* 76, no. 276 (2012), 386.

and boosting the economy.[2] As already noted, Christians' refusal to participate in the patriotic pagan celebrations made them easy marks for social ostracism and accusations of atheism.

The New Testament shows an ever-present tension between Christians and Jewish populations throughout the empire. Jews viewed the Christian doctrine of grace to be an oversimplification and gross distortion of Jewish law. Initially viewed as a Jewish subset, Christianity enjoyed "a degree of protection under [its] umbrella" and they were not forced to participate in the imperial cult.[3] Under Nero's reign, heavy persecution of Christians motivated Jews to put distance between themselves and the nascent religious movement, keeping themselves from the same fate. Non-participation by Christians in cult practices drove yet another wedge between them and the Jewish community. Beale notes that Jews sometimes "had no qualms in semi-revering other deities along with their Old Testament God."[4] They argued that Christian avoidance of pagan rituals and celebrations was a significant mark of distinction, illustrating that Christianity was not a Jewish sect. In Smyrna, Jews were a contributing factor to the suffering Christians endured.

Fear and anxiety describe daily life for Christians in Smyrna, yet they persevered. Facing increasing pressure to compromise their beliefs, the Smyrnaean church stood firm in their conviction that there is no Lord but Christ. Their position caused no small amount of suffering—even to the point of death. Now, Jesus sends a message of comfort in the midst of their suffering.

---

2   *ibid*, 388, note 11.
3   Beale, *Revelation*, 240.
4   *ibid*.

Death is Not the End

Jesus greets the Smyrnaean church as "the first and the last," reminding them of His eternality. The first words of the Bible ("In the beginning, God created…") assert God's existence before there was a beginning. John opens his gospel record with similar phrasing: "In the beginning was the Word." He then argues explicitly that the Word is Jesus Himself, writing, "and the Word became flesh and dwelt among us."[5] The Word was God, and God became flesh and dwelt among us. The Word is Jesus, and He was present and active before there was a beginning. He is the first and the last, existing before time and long after time itself comes to an end. Victories and successes come and go; defeats and failures come and go; times of prosperity and suffering come and go. Jesus remains the same "yesterday and today and forever."[6] Jesus reminds the Smyrnaeans that He has not left nor has His power diminished. Jesus was I AM before Rome ever was, and He remains long after it passed into history.

When considering eternity, death loses some of its fear-invoking potency. Jesus, the eternal One, died, but He came back to life three days later. Death could not hold Him. The same people who saw Jesus's body interred also walked and talked with Him afterwards. Paul wrote that Jesus appeared to Peter and the apostles and to "more than five hundred brethren at one time, most of whom remain until now."[7] The fact of Jesus's resurrection energized everyone who saw Him. It confirmed His claims of Sonship as well as His promise of eternal life for all who believe and follow Him. "If Christ has not been raised," Paul continues, "then our preaching is vain, your faith also is vain…But Christ has been raised from

---

5   John 1:1, 14.
6   Hebrews 13:8.
7   1 Corinthians 15:5-7.

the dead, the first fruits of those who are asleep."[8] The resurrection
was everything. It still is.

Jesus being the "first fruits of those who are asleep" means that
every Christian will one day rise again to be with Him. Indeed,
Revelation records a time when death itself comes to an end. In
Smyrna, death lurked in the shadows, but Christians need never
fear because Jesus conquered death and the grave. His victory is
our victory. Death is not the end. It is but a milestone marking our
transition into eternity.

By referencing His own suffering, death, and resurrection,
Christ connects His own experience with that of the Smyrna. The
Greek historian, Herodotus, notes that the Lydian king, Alyattes
(r. 610-560 BCE), sacked Smyrna then razed it to the ground.[9] For
almost two hundred years, the city remained virtually uninhabited.
Successors to Alexander the Great, Antigonus I and Lysimachus,
rebuilt Smyrna around 400 BCE, fulfilling Alexander's plan to
return the city to its former glory. Smyrna's rising from the ashes
inspired the use of the phoenix as the city's symbol. Jesus connects
to that pathos, identifying Himself as the One who died and rose
again. His experience marks Himself as one of them, as one who—
like a phoenix—also rose from the ashes.

Isn't that just like Jesus, though? He seems to go out of His
way to let us know He understands us. He is not a far-off Savior,
observing His followers from a distance. Instead, He is among
His flock; He stands amid the lampstands. Christ is intimately
acquainted with each of us as a person. Through His life and death,
Jesus fully understands physical suffering, persecution, and emotional
hardship. Through His resurrection, Jesus gives hope of eternal,
abundant life to His followers. Rather than assert authority, Jesus

8   1 Corinthians 15:13, 20.
9   Herodotus, *The Histories,* trans. Tom Holland, (1.15-16).

references His suffering as qualification to comfort the Church. *You're suffering,* He might say, *I have also suffered. I was dead and have come to life.* A wonderful and timely message both then and now from our Lord and our Hope.

Can you feel the intimacy and emotion of Jesus's greeting? Can you identify with His suffering? With Smyrna's? Jesus knows you, all of you—your pain, your struggles, and your history. He understands who you are and how you came to be who you are. This is more than knowing you before you were formed in the womb. The Lord understands who you are right now, and He understands *why* you are right now. He understands all your history, all your decisions, all your successes and failures and tragedies and triumphs that brought you to this point. Hebrews tells us that Jesus was "tempted in all things as we are, yet without sin."[10] There is no reason to fear His gaze. He sees what others can't see, and He knows what others don't know. He sees *you.* He knows *you.*

Christianity and Suffering

Oh, to live in a world in which suffering didn't exist! How great would it be if Jesus (as our Good Shepherd) protected people from any sort of suffering? The problem is that Jesus never so much as suggested an end to suffering on this side of eternity. Instead, He said things like, "You will be hated by all because of My name."[11] Suffering cannot be separated from Christianity, nor does suffering suggest faithlessness or spiritual failure. On the contrary, suffering teaches us a lot about ourselves, about the Lord, and about the relationship between us. Suffering is a theology. The life Jesus promises is not abundant because there is no struggle. It's abundant because it's full of Him. We tend to treat suffering and

---

10   Hebrews 4:15.
11   Matthew 10:22.

God's love as opposite ends of a spectrum (like grace and truth in the previous chapter). But it is often *in* suffering that we experience the love of God more fully, more powerfully. Smyrna understood that. They suffered every day.

Jesus Commends Suffering

Jesus's consolation to the Smyrnaean church commends their steadfast faith in spite of constant persecution. Beale notes that participation "to some degree" in emperor-worship opened doors for prosperity and social standing.[12] Although it would have been advantageous for them, Christians in Smyrna refused to adopt any aspect of cult or pagan practices. Instead, they chose hardship, poverty, and social marginalization. The Ephesians allowed hardship to harden their hearts. In contrast, the Smyrnaeans chose to follow the model set by the apostles who, after being arrested and beaten for preaching Jesus, "went on their way…*rejoicing* that they had been considered worthy to suffer shame for His name."[13] For the apostles, suffering indicated victory, not defeat. It was not something to be avoided but celebrated. Like the apostles, the Smyrnaean believers embraced suffering because it aligned with the work of Christ, and Jesus commended them for it.

The Greek words translated "tribulation" and "poverty" in verse nine add incredible depth to our understanding of life for Christians in Smyrna. *Thlipsis* (**thlip**-sis) is translated as "tribulation" twenty-one times in the New Testament and "affliction" seventeen times. It is the adjective form of the word meaning "to press" or "press hard upon," like in a winepress or an oil press. The use of *thlipsis* here, then, gestures back toward Gethsemane on the Mount of Olives. Gethsemane literally means "an oil press" and is the place

---

12   Beale, *Revelation*, 240.
13   Acts 5:41, emphasis mine.

where Jesus prayed under such strain that the Son of God sweat drops of blood. "And being in agony," Luke records in his gospel record, "He was praying very fervently; and His sweat became like drops of blood, falling down upon the ground."[14] *Thlipsis* describes constant hardship, constant pressure, constant strain that slowly squeezes life out of someone. Jesus knew their tribulation. He also knew their poverty.

There are two words in the Greek which translate to "poor" or "poverty" in the New Testament. The first is *penes* (**pen**-ace), and it describes anyone who needs to work for a living, regardless of how much they make. The wealthy in the Greco-Roman world had servants. If you didn't have servants, you were considered *penes*, poor. The word Jesus uses, though, is *pthocheia* (pto-**khi**-ah), which literally translates as "beggary," suggesting Smyrnaean Christians suffered from abject poverty. They were not simply poor, living hand to mouth (or paycheck to paycheck). Rather, they were made to carry the heavy burden of destitution reducing them to begging in order to survive. Once again, we see a life closely resembling that of Christ. My pastor often said, "Jesus needed to borrow a penny for an object lesson. Now that is poor!"[15] Matthew records Jesus turning away would-be followers, saying, "The Son of Man has nowhere to lay His head."[16] If we're following Jesus to escape poverty or hardship, we're going to be very frustrated very quickly.

In their suffering and in their poverty, the Smyrnaean believers lived very much like Jesus, their Lord. As wonderful as that sounds, when faithfulness produces long periods of suffering or the loss of everything, words of encouragement can shrink to mere platitudes in our minds, empty clichés salting our wounds. Imagine the crushing

---

14   Luke 22:44.
15   This reference is from Jesus's "render unto Caesar" teaching found in Matthew 22, Mark 12, and Luke 20.
16   Matthew 8:20.

oppression the Smyrnaean church lived under day after day. Now imagine their relief in knowing their perseverance had not gone unseen and that they were not alone. And this is only the beginning of the letter.

The parenthetical "but you are rich" asserts that God measures wealth by a different standard than the world, by something other than money or possessions, influence or power. The Smyrnaean church had none of those things, yet Jesus declared they were rich. They possessed something Jesus called "true riches."[17] Sounds great, right? That is, until we're the ones living in *pthocheia*. Wouldn't more money have made the Smyrnaean Christians feel better, giving them financial security in a world bent on ensuring their insecurity? Maybe. But for how long? How much wealth would be "enough" for them to feel secure? How much would it be for us? Perhaps this is why Jesus does not promise them financial prosperity, even though He knew and saw their abject poverty. Jesus's solution to poverty is not more money, it's more of Himself. It sounds contradictory, but it perfectly describes wealth in the context of eternity.

Jesus's teachings imply a difference in the wealth we can obtain here in life and the wealth we will obtain in heaven. In the Sermon on the Mount, Jesus exhorts His audience not to focus on storing wealth here on earth, "where moth and rust destroy," but to "store up for yourselves treasures in heaven…for where your treasure is, there your heart will be also."[18] In that same message, Jesus calls wealth and God "masters," asserting that it is impossible to serve both because they each require undivided loyalty. Smyrna stands as an example of serving God rather than wealth. Their decision to follow Jesus may have resulted in earthly poverty and trials, but they never faltered, because it also meant fellowship with Christ

---

17   Luke 16:11.
18   Matthew 6:19-20.

and wealth in the heavenly realm. They focused on Christ *as* their treasure, rooting their heart in heaven. Christians may seem like poor, rejected outsiders, but they are in fact seen and loved by Christ, embraced as children of God, possessing eternal wealth in heaven. To be sure, the Smyrnaeans were not unaffected by their financial circumstances, but Christ's words of comfort here provide a moment of sweet relief.

Have you ever gone through a hardship that you felt nobody understood? Did you feel unnoticed and unseen in those times? Have you thought that perhaps God either didn't know or—worse—couldn't be bothered to care? The church in Smyrna suffered tribulation and abject poverty for years. Years! No one came to their aid. Neither government nor society rallied to their side as allies fighting the injustices against them. The apparent isolation would make it very easy for the Smyrnaean church to believe they were being punished, that God had struck them for some unknown immorality. When suffering lasts that long, it can feel as though God doesn't see what we're going through. Jesus's commendations to the church in Smyrna reassures us that He does. He may not relieve our suffering, but He lets us know we are not alone in it.

Jesus Implies More Suffering

Rather than comfort Smyrna with the promise of ending their suffering, Jesus instead indicates that their suffering was about to increase. "Do not fear what you're about to suffer," He says, with layers of foreshadowing. As if poverty, oppression, social marginalization, and the threat of exile or worse were not enough, Jesus informs them more is coming. He mentions that some will be thrown into prison (a Roman prison was often a holding area for executions), while others will be harshly interrogated and goaded into rejecting Christ. He notes they will experience "tribulation for ten days."[19] Some scholars suggest "ten days" borrows from the "language of the arena" since games were prevalent in Smyrna.[20] According to Grant Osborn, games "would be especially dangerous times of anti-Christian sentiment."[21] The term indicates a short but intense period of persecution with the strong possibility of death. "The persecution will rage for a time," Ramsay writes, "but it will not be permanent."[22]

In John's Gospel, we read where Jesus spoke about the juxtaposition of suffering and faith: "The thief [indicating Satan] comes only to steal and kill and destroy; I came that they [indicating believers] may have life, and have it abundantly."[23] How do we reconcile Jesus's promise of abundant life for all believers with His promise of increased suffering for the believers in Smyrna? Apparently, abundance means something entirely different to Jesus than it does to the rest of the world. Christ saw the poverty and suffering of the Smyrnaean church and held it in high esteem, without a single word of rebuke for it. Wiersbe writes, "They may not have enjoyed the approval of men, but they certainly received the praise of God."[24] Smyrna suffered well, enduring hardships, trusting Jesus, and continuing to preach the gospel with their lives as well as their words. Jesus considered their life of suffering—as difficult as it was—to be abundant. Abundance is not found in our surroundings, our achievements, or our bank accounts. Abundance is only found in Jesus Himself. He is our great reward.

It would not take long for Jesus's promise of increased suffering to be fulfilled. The Greek historian, Eusebius, writes that the entire

---

19   Revelation 2:10.
20   Colin J. Hemer, *The Letters to the Seven Churches of Asia in Their Local Setting* (Grand Rapids, MI; Cambridge, U.K.; Livonia, MI: William B Eerdmans Publishing Company; Dove Booksellers, 2001), p. 69.
21   Osborne, *Revelation*, 133.
22   Ramsay, *The Letters to the Seven Churches*, 275.
23   John 10:10.
24   Wiersbe, *The Bible Exposition Commentary*, 573.

region of Asia Minor descended into "the most savage persecutions" under the reign of Antoninus and Lucius, leading to the "fulfillment in martyrdom" of one of the most well-known Smyrnaeans: Polycarp.[25] Polycarp was a disciple of John and may have been in attendance when this letter was read. Being a student of John's, Polycarp adopted the same allergy to compromise. So, when the state began forcing Christians to participate in the imperial cult, Polycarp's days were numbered. Eusebius includes a letter from the Smyrnaean church recounting Polycarp's martyrdom.

> *He was met by Herod the chief of police and his father Nicetes, who, after transferring him to their carriage, sat beside him and tried persuasion. "What harm is there in saying, 'Lord Caesar' and sacrificing?*

Polycarp faced death by any number of gruesome methods (he was burned at the stake). Surely, he could be excused for saying a few words and making a token offering to appease the crowd, saving his life to continue ministering, right? Once Polycarp arrived at the stadium filled with blood-thirsty onlookers, the proconsul overseeing the day's events also tried to persuade him to save his own life.

> *"Swear by Caesar's fortune; change your attitude ... Swear, and I will set you free: execrate Christ!" Polycarp replied, "For eighty-six years I have been His servant, and He has never done me wrong: how can I blaspheme my King who saved me?"[26]*

Polycarp looked over his decades of service to—and suffering for—Jesus and concluded that Christ had never done him wrong. Certainly, Polycarp had a fundamentally different definition of "abundant" than we do, and he was not alone. Through the years, and into our own time, countless men and women have gladly given

---

25   Eusebius, *Histories* (4.15), p. 117.
26   *ibid*, p. 119-120.

their lives, suffering horrific deaths rather than recant their faith in Jesus as the Son of God and Savior of the world.

Today, Christians expend incredible energy to avoid hardship, protecting against poverty, and fighting against perceived persecution. How different we are from those first followers of Jesus! The root of that difference is found in our definition of terms and our expectations of Christ. Jesus never promised a life filled with perpetual promotion and progress. Instead, He warned, "In the world you have tribulation, but take courage; I have overcome the world."[27] Something the first-century Church understood was that Jesus is not about making His people wealthy in this world. His goal is not to allow us to live comfortably and retire earlier. Jesus came into the world to seek and save the lost. His singular goal is bringing dead souls to life.

So, I have to ask: why have we come to Jesus? Why did we give Him the pieces of our lives? Did we hope He would take them and create a new life that was vastly improved and more comfortable *now*? Early Christians embraced Jesus because they recognized their own sinfulness, and they understood a Savior was required for redemption, declaring Jesus as that Savior. Coming to Jesus for any other reason results in frustration: we pray, and our prayers don't get answered; we expect, and our expectations don't get met; we set a bar for God, and He laughs. The life Jesus creates with our pieces may not be more comfortable, but that's because our new life is meant to glorify God. Early Christians understood that, even embraced it, considering martyrdom a "fulfillment" of their faith.[28]

Success and prosperity and abundance carry different meanings in the Kingdom of God because they are rooted in the Kingdom

---

27   John 16:33.
28   Eusebius calls Polycarp's martyrdom a "fulfillment" of his faith in *Histories* (4.15), p. 117.

of God. Jesus alludes to this at the beginning of the letter by identifying Himself as the One who "was dead and has come to life." Toward the end of it, Jesus encourages the Smyrnaean church to "be faithful until death, and I will give you the crown of life," focusing their eyes on a point in space and time beyond their current circumstances, even beyond the present world. The fact that Jesus rose from the dead confirms there is, indeed, life after death. Jesus wants His Church to look toward *that* life, living in such a way that confirms belief in that life, and making decisions that carry implications for that life. We experience the promises of God in part now, trusting that we will experience them in full in that life.

Jesus Promises Eternal Life

Jesus indicates rewards await His followers once they leave this life and begin their eternity with Him in heaven. To the Smyrnaeans, Jesus promised a crown of life to all who are faithful unto death. James (who many consider to be the brother of Jesus) also notes that the crown of life will be given to all who "persevere under trial," suggesting the crown of life will be given to those who die for their faith.[29] The significance of the crown was not lost on the Smyrnaeans, who hosted athletic games each year in which athletes competed for a victor's laurel, or crown. Paul alludes to this, asserting that both athletes and Christians "exercise self-control in all things"—athletes for "a corruptible crown," but Christians for "an incorruptible" crown.[30] The crown signifies victory. The rest of the world may consider martyrdom a pointless loss, an unmitigated defeat, but the crown of life is awarded to those who lose their lives because of their faith. Death, in this context, is victory.

---

29   James 1:12.
30   1 Corinthians 9:25, KJV.

Life does not end when this life ends. Jesus proved that. With Jesus's tomb sealed, the Romans thought they had gotten rid of a troublemaker, the Jewish authorities thought they had gotten rid of a blasphemer, the devil thought he had killed the Son of God. They were all wrong. Jesus rose from the dead, proving that death is merely a finish line (to borrow Paul's sports analogy) marking the end of our race and the beginning of eternal life with Him. Coming near the end of his life, Paul wrote Timothy these stirring words:

> I have fought the good fight, I have finished the course, I have kept the faith; in the future there is laid up for me the crown of righteousness, which the Lord, the righteous Judge, will award to me on that day; and not only to me, but also to all who have loved His appearing.[31]

Dear friend, keep fighting the good fight. Keep the faith and strive for the crowns waiting for you in heaven.

To everyone who overcomes, Jesus promises they "will not be hurt by the second death."[32] I used to believe that only Christians live forever. I was wrong. All of us will live forever. Regardless of our faith or lack of faith, regardless of which god we believe in or if we believe there is no God, all of us will live forever. The only question is where we will spend it. What is our eternal destination? Jesus's promise to be kept from the second death is the first use of the term in the Bible. It is a foreboding expression that gets explained later in Revelation, when John writes, "Then death and Hades were thrown into the lake of fire. This is the second death, the lake of fire. And if anyone's name was not found in the book of life, he was thrown into the lake of fire."[33] The second death is the eternal torment Jesus often alluded to in His ministry.

---

31   2 Timothy 4:7-8.
32   Revelation 2:11.
33   Revelation 20:14-15.

Christians faced execution in horrific manners, including being burned alive. Jesus assures them (and us) that even though His followers may be tortured and killed in this life, they won't be touched by the second death in the next life. Paul's declaration to the Romans feels especially appropriate here: "The wages of sin is death, but the free gift of God is eternal life in Christ Jesus our Lord."[34]

Life for Smyrnaean Christians was one of poverty, tribulation, suffering, and death. There was no hope to come out from it because that's just the way it was. Jesus confirmed that, telling them their suffering would continue and actually worsen. But He also comforts them by asserting things are not what they seem. We may not have much in terms of wealth and possessions, but true wealth is not found in this life; it is found in the next. We may be poor in this world, but if we are following Jesus, we are spiritually rich and are living an abundant life. We may suffer now, but "now" is not all there is. We may even die because of our faith, but that's not defeat—it's victory, and we will receive a reward.

Hold fast, overcome, and you will see Jesus on the other side.

---

34   Romans 6:23.

Revelation 2:12–17

12 *"And to the angel of the church in Pergamum write: The One who has the sharp two-edged sword says this:*

13 *'I know where you dwell, where Satan's throne is; and you hold fast My name, and did not deny My faith even in the days of Antipas, My witness, My faithful one, who was killed among you, where Satan dwells.*

14 *'But I have a few things against you, because you have there some who hold the teaching of Balaam, who kept teaching Balak to put a stumbling block before the sons of Israel, to eat things sacrificed to idols and to commit acts of immorality.*

15 *'So you also have some who in the same way hold the teaching of the Nicolaitans.*

16 *'Therefore repent; or else I am coming to you quickly, and I will make war against them with the sword of My mouth.*

17 *'He who has an ear, let him hear what the Spirit says to the churches. To him who overcomes, to him I will give some of the hidden manna, and I will give him a white stone, and a new name written on the stone which no one knows but he who receives it.'*

Chapter 4
The Letter to Pergamum

L ike Ephesus and Smyrna, Pergamum was a city of great wealth and was highly esteemed. It served as the capital of the Roman province of Asia and a center for the imperial cult. Additionally, a large hill dominated the landscape of the city, upon which were built a number of temples to various Greco-Roman deities, including Zeus (god of victory), Athena (goddess of war), Asclepios (god of healing), and Dionysos (god of the grape-harvest and winemaking). The royal family of Pergamum claimed to be descended from Dionysos.[1] Indeed, Pergamum was like all other cities in the region (including the seven to whom Jesus sent His revelation), with a large variety of religions all vying for the hearts, minds, and money of the people. What set Pergamum apart, however, was its relationship to knowledge and the written word.

A Relationship with the Word

Reaching the height of its glory in the second and third century BCE, Pergamum was home to the second largest library in the

---

1   Ramsay, *The Letters to the Seven Churches*, 284.

world. The city is also credited with innovating the use of animal skins instead of papyrus plant as a writing medium, coining the term *pergamēn* "parchment."[2] Jesus gestures toward this distinction, drawing attention to the power of *His* Word and the efficacy of *His* doctrine, introducing Himself as "the One who has the sharp two-edged sword."[3]

In chapter one, we discussed the meaning behind the two-edged sword coming from the mouth of Jesus. We also examined how Hebrews compares the Word of God to a sword, describing it as "living and active and sharper than any two-edged sword."[4] While a physical sword can pierce a literal heart, the Word of God pierces our spiritual heart, exposing its thoughts and intentions. Painful, but when wielded by the Holy Spirit, the Word brings life and healing, strengthening our faith. The image of the sword-wielding Christ comes again toward the end of Revelation, where we see Jesus "striking down nations" with the sharp sword coming from His mouth.[5] It is this writer's opinion that the message conveyed is clear: in the current age, the Word of God chastens and corrects; but in the coming age, the Word of God will strike down and destroy. God's Word is not benign. It is powerful, possessing the authority of God Himself.

Jesus's introduction draws attention to the power of His Word, signaling His intention to make His Word the focal point of this letter. The influences surrounding the church in Pergamos were not unique to them. Political, religious, and social forces converged on

---

2   Some historians believe animal skins were used by the Egyptians in the second millennium BCE. Other writers, like commentator William Barclay, describe a contention between Egypt and Pergamum in the third century BCE that led to the innovation of parchment in Pergamum. Either way, the extensive number of parchments housed by the library in Pergamum (over 200,000 according to Barclay) may have led to the term "*pergamēn*" in the first or second century BCE. See William Barclay, *The Revelation of John*, 88.

3   Revelation 2:12.

4   Hebrews 4:12.

5   Revelation 19:15.

all believers, leaving them to make a choice: compromise and live, or remain faithful to Christ and perhaps lose everything, including your life. As we'll see further in this chapter, Pergamum had some whose faith was showing signs of cracking. Beginning this letter by highlighting the two-edged sword emphasizes Jesus's desire for His Church to be a people of His Word.

This seems to be a good time to ask: how tightly are you holding on to God's Word? How often do you not only read the Bible, but pour yourself into the teachings of Jesus? Our lives are filled with many voices vying for our attention, producing a cacophony and drowning out the still small voice of the Lord. Some messages sound good, but are merely well-produced counterfeits, whose only intention is to remove Jesus from the narrative. The only protection against lies and forgeries is consistent handling of the truth (or, perhaps more correctly, knowing the Truth personally). God's Word is truth. Jesus Himself is truth.

It's Not Where You Live, but How You Live

Believers in Pergamum were literally surrounded by religions, cultures, and governments that were at times anti-Christ but always antagonistic toward Christianity. Yet, even in the worst circumstances, they held on to Jesus and His Word. Even today, we see similar scenarios playing out all over the world. For example, the church in China thrives against the relentless oppression of the Chinese government; believers in Muslim-majority countries face the possibility of death, yet they are some of the most faithful, loving, evangelical people I have ever had the honor of meeting. Here in the United States, Christians enjoy a privileging of their religious principles—so much so, that many believe we were founded as a Christian nation. However, the centering of Christianity in our culture has not produced a people with a stronger faith or a more steadfast hold on the Word of God. Indeed, an argument can be made that privilege has produced a markedly *opposite* effect. Faithfulness does not spring from environment. It comes, first, from a desire to remain faithful to the Lord, then from choosing daily to follow Him and live according to His Word. It takes incredible energy and comes at a great cost, but it is possible to hold on to the Word of Christ and maintain faith in Him in any and all circumstances.

Christ describes Pergamum as the city where Satan's throne (or "seat," depending on your translation) is and where Satan dwells, indicating an intense—almost dangerous—cultural environment. Warren Wiersbe suggests Satan's throne signifies the worship of Asclepios, "whose insignia was the entwined serpent on the staff."[6] To be sure, the temple of Asclepios served as a proto-hospital, and people throughout the empire came to the city for healing. And while Pergamum certainly drew thousands with its myriad temples to various deities, it is unlikely that Jesus referred to pagan worship as Satan's throne. Nor is it likely that Christ compared Zeus, Athena, Asclepios, or any other pagan deity to Satan since doing so would give them viability, suggesting they exist. Instead, calling Pergamum the place where Satan's seat is located gestures toward the city as being the seat of power for the empire in Asia Minor. The pressure upon Christians to conform to the Roman way of life (including worship) would have been severe. Yet, Jesus indicates they held fast to His name, never denying their faith in Him.

"I know where you dwell," Jesus tells them. The cultural tension in which they lived was not lost on Jesus: He knew the circumstances surrounding them, and the persecution and violence they endured. It's impossible to overstate the pervasiveness of the

---

6   Wiersbe, *The Bible Exposition Commentary*, 573.

imperial cult in cities like Pergamum. Add to that, the Acropolis-esque hill dominated by various temples invited worshipers to the city. Tucked inside this swirling milieu was a tiny group of Christians. Jesus commends their willingness to hold fast to His name when it would have been beneficial to renounce it. Jesus values faithfulness, and faithfulness shines in darkness. His requirement of faithfulness does not vary based on where we live. To be sure, the Pergamum church was tested daily. Yet, their faith never wavered, even when Antipas, one of their members, was executed.

By mentioning Antipas's martyrdom specifically, Jesus acknowledges their pain and validates their grief. Antipas, and by extension the church, was both seen and known by Christ in both life and death. Jesus describes Antipas as "My witness, My faithful one."[7] It is a beautiful moment in the letter where Jesus claims Antipas as His own, giving him a title (witness) similar to the one He holds Himself (faithful and true witness).[8] Antipas's death was not in vain, nor did it go unnoticed. "Precious in the sight of the Lord," the psalmist wrote, "is the death of His saints."[9] Like Satan at the cross, Rome thought it had the last word with Antipas. Jesus proves them wrong. Barclay gives an insightful explanation here:

> Roman governors were divided into two classes – those who had the ius gladii, the right of the sword, and those who had not. Those who had the right of the sword had the power of life and death; on their word a man could be executed on the spot. Humanly speaking the proconsul, who had his headquarters in Pergamum, had the ius gladii...and at any moment he might use it against any Christian; but the letter bids the Christian not to forget that last word is still with the Risen Christ, who has the sharp two-edged sword.[10]

---

7   Revelation 2:13.
8   See Revelation 1:5 and 3:14.
9   Psalm 116:15.
10   Barclay, *Revelation*, 90.

There is no disputing the power of the Roman empire or the authority of its many governors and military leaders. This letter reminded Pergamum that however mighty the prevailing forces against Christ and His people may become, Jesus is far greater. That is still true today. Jesus is still the name that is above every other name. Nothing in heaven or earth can ever change that.

The Pergamum church stands as part of the cloud of witnesses for our current age. Modern Christians tend to believe the Church faces persecution like never before, that spiritual forces have ramped up their rhetoric and their attacks on the body of Christ. The rallying cry of, "We're living in the last days!" is meant to give credence to this belief. Yet, what we face today is no worse than what the Church (or any people of God) has faced at any other time or place. The pressure to conform never relents, it only undulates, rising and falling with the times. Culture changes, governments change, even nations come and go. Only Christ and His Word remains unchanged. Isaiah wrote, "The grass withers [the people are grass], the flower fades, but the word of our God stands forever."[11]

Christ calls His followers to live differently from the rest of the world. That was the point of His entire teaching ministry. He constantly subverted religious tradition that ignored the Spirit of the law while obsessing over its letter. He taught that His followers would be known for their love rather than adherence to any particular set of regulations. If Christians are governed by any law, it is the law of love. However, if we are not careful, world events, cultural changes, and circumstances of life will combine to produce a powerful magnetic force drawing us away from Christ's law. Rather than responding with love, in faith, we will respond in kind: anger for anger, hate for hate, violence for violence.

---

11   Isaiah 40:4.

Jesus Warns Against Compromise

Jesus commends the Pergamum believers for *not* conforming to the myriad powers pulling against them, choosing instead to be "transformed by the renewing of their mind."[12] Christianity was a tiny, relatively unknown sect of Judaism, surrounded by multiple religions and paganism in its various forms. How difficult it must have been to live a life of faith in Christ as the Son of God and Savior of the world. Yet, they remained steadfast amidst incredible persecution, and Jesus saw them.

Although the church in Pergamum (as a whole) maintained their faith and held on to the name of Christ, Jesus indicated there were some who privately adopted the false teachings promoted around them. The problem was not that misguided or non-believing people were in the church. To be sure, the church is exactly where Christ wants any of us who hold beliefs that vary from His word. Instead, Christ's warning suggests there was no corrective action being taken in the church, no formative doctrine being taught to counter the false doctrine held by some. Whereas the Ephesians militantly guarded themselves against false teaching, ejecting anyone who held such doctrine, the church at Pergamum did nothing. That is dangerous.

If there were people in our churches today who firmly held erroneous beliefs (racism, for example), we would expect some sort of corrective action: a private conversation with the pastor, perhaps, or a sermon (or even a segment within a sermon) addressing racism and promoting the universal equality of all people as the Lord's image bearers. What we would *not* expect (and what I hope we never accept) is inaction. A little leaven leavens the whole lump.[13] Silence

---

12 Romans 12:2.
13 Paul used this colloquialism to emphasize the need for ensuring sound doctrine within the church, exhorting the Corinthian church to purge the old leaven to keep it from spreading.

is agreement, and agreement promotes proliferation. Generally, the Pergamum church remained faithful, but some members were beginning to bend under the unrelenting cultural pressures. It was a moment that called for action, not silence.

What, exactly, was the false teaching Jesus so emphatically warned against? In a word: compromise. The story of Balaam (to which Jesus refers) is one of compromise.[14] The book of Numbers records when King Balak of Moab found the Israelite army encamped against his people. Fearing for his life and that of his kingdom, Balak sent for Balaam, a well-known Edomite prophet, to come and curse Israel. The Lord forbade Balaam from doing this (obviously), so he instead counseled Balak to entice Israle to compromise their beliefs, suggesting Balak offer Moabite women as wives for Israel. In the words of the Jewish historian, Josephus, their wives would convince them "to leave off their obedience to their own laws and the worship of that God who established them, and to worship the gods of the Midianites and Moabites; *for by this means God will be angry at them.*"[15] Balak's army could not defeat Israel, but if the king was patient, Israel's God would do it for him. It worked. The very first commandments forbid having or worshiping any other gods. Yet, Israel "ate and bowed down to their [Moabite] gods" and "joined themselves to Baal of Peor, and the Lord was angry against" them.[16] The teaching of Balaam begins with small compromises but ends with destruction.

Some in the Pergamum church had begun participating in the local and imperial pagan ceremonies as well as committing "acts of immorality," holding to the teachings of Balaam and the Nicolaitans. Beale suggests those compromised believers argued their acts were simply "empty gestures that fulfilled patriotic or

14   You can read Balaam's story in full in Numbers 22-25.
15   Josephus, *The Works of Josephus,* 111 (emphasis mine).
16   Numbers 25:2-3.

social obligations."[17] For them, these small acts held no spiritual significance since Christians are set free from the law of sin and death. Jesus disagrees. Compromises to our faith—no matter how small—are stumbling blocks meant to cause God's people to fall. While God may not respond the way He did in the Old Testament, fall enough times and our internal monologue adds its voice to the many others enticing us to walk away from Jesus. How many times have we heard people say, "I tried church, but it didn't work for me." Instead of "doing" church, Christians are called to follow Jesus. He alone is the way, truth, and life. Anything that deviates from Him is a stumbling block.

Christians today face similar temptations to compromise. Worldly wisdom compels us to adopt cultural principles that run counter to God's Word, arguing it will make the Church (and Christians) more relevant. Christians are often encouraged to blend ideologies, philosophies, theories, and various religious beliefs, creating an entirely new gospel that is not a gospel at all. These arguments equate relevance with effectiveness. In other words, if we want to reach the world with the gospel, we have to become a bit like the world. However, Paul argued that *only* the gospel is the power of God for salvation.[18] There are various ways to declare and receive the gospel, but only one gospel message. If we were to ask a dozen Christians how they came to know Jesus as Lord and Savior, we would hear twelve different stories with a common denominator: Jesus.

Jesus is the gospel.

There is no good news (in an eternal context) outside of Christ. Adding or removing anything to the gospel produces an entirely new thing with no salvific power. However relevant to the culture it

---

17   Beale, *The Book of Revelation*, 249.
18   Romans 1:16.

might be, it is no longer the power of God to salvation. I have heard some people adopt the phrase "All roads lead to Rome," to argue that there are many roads leading to heaven. The New Testament writers present a different argument: many roads lead to Jesus, but Jesus is the only road to the Father and eternity in heaven.

When culture or society or our family, friends, neighbors, or coworkers endorse, exhort, or demand compromise, hold fast. When religious or denominational tradition tries to add anything to the finished work of Jesus, diminishing the power of His sacrifice, stand firm. Jesus is the Christ. He is the Way, the Truth, and the Life. Like first-century believers, we, too, must intentionally hold fast to what we know of Jesus:

> For indeed Jews ask for signs and Greeks search for wisdom; but we preach Christ crucified, to Jews a stumbling block and to Gentiles foolishness, but to those who are the called, both Jews and Greeks, Christ the power of God and the wisdom of God.[19]

There is only one way to heaven, and it's Christ, crucified. There's only one road to eternal life: Christ—the Messiah of God and Savior of the world—crucified. He finished the work required for salvation. Everything else is a stumbling block. There is nothing else Jesus can do—nothing else He *will* do—for our salvation. We can't bargain our way into heaven, telling Jesus that we will follow Him *if* He heals, or *if* He gives, or *if* He performs a miracle. That dog won't hunt. The only sacrifice acceptable by God for our sins is the death of Jesus, His Son; and *that* work is finished. Hold fast. Jesus refuses to budge when it comes to compromise, regardless of our ~~reason~~ excuse for it.[20] In a clash of dueling doctrines, the two-edged sword of Jesus ultimately prevails.

---

19   1 Corinthians 1:22–24.
20   The strikethrough is intentional. To quote my pastor: "Excuses are just lies in disguise."

Ready or Not, Jesus Is Coming

Notice that Jesus promises His coming to the church ("I am coming to you"), but His war will be against heretics within the church ("I will make war against them").[21] That Jesus makes war with the sword of His mouth does not indicate a war of words. The coming battle is not the final end-boss fight between the gospel and whatever ideology might be prevailing at the time. The war Jesus indicates here is a bloody, horrifically one-sided war where everyone Jesus comes against dies.[22]

As with all seven churches (symbolizing the entirety of Christ's Church), Jesus's solution is repentance, a complete turn-around in response to Christ's revelation. For the church, it meant speaking out against heretical teaching rather than remaining silent as, to value every single person as a sheep in Christ's flock and protect them from harmful doctrines. For the individual believers, it meant seriously evaluating their faith, ensuring it was firmly grounded in Christ alone. His warning suggests that both the church and individual members of the church are accountable for their actions (or inactions). This sounds harsh, but the alternative is worse. Remaining silent signals acceptance of those teachings as proper, putting people's eternity at risk. Pergamum's repentance, then, is not solely for its own benefit, but for all who are following a gerrymandered gospel.

The call for Pergamum's repentance stands perfectly in line with Jesus's teaching and that of the entire New Testament, namely the giving of self for the benefit of others. "The Son of Man did not come to be served," Jesus told His followers, "but to serve, and to give His life a ransom for many."[23] Jesus calls Pergamum

---

21   Revelation 2:16.
22   Seriously, it's gruesome. See Revelation 19:11-21.
23   Matthew 20:28.

to set aside personal comfort for the sake of those bound to suffer by the sword of Christ's Word. Repentance did not necessarily benefit the Pergamum church, who were already holding fast the name of Christ, but it carried the possibility of saving others. Our actions never only affect ourselves. In this case, the benefactors of Pergamum's repentance are those caught in a web of deceit, living in a way that seems wise but the end of which is destruction.

I don't want to make repentance sound easy. It never is. There is always a cost to repentance, but the benefits mitigate the difficulty and cost associated with it. Like Ephesus, the cultural response of the church in Pergamum lacked balance. Ephesus gravitated toward truth, fiercely guarding against heresy, but compromising their first love. Pergamum chose silence when faced with false doctrine in the church. They prioritized grace, but it was a cheap grace that cost nothing. Speaking against heresy at Pergamum would strain relational connections, perhaps resulting in the loss of members and close friends.[24] However, the cost of repentance is much less than the cost of doing nothing (as we will see in the next chapter), and the reward for repentance is always worth the price.

A Feast for Overcomers

When considering what it means to overcome the world, we have to admit that none of us are perfect, nor do any of us live in a spiritual utopia, free from outside influences. All of us are called to overcome because all of us face things that need to be overcome. However, no matter how difficult this life becomes, Christ's promises give us hope. For those who choose God's Word over the world, Jesus's promises provide sweet consolation. They remind us that one

---

24   Although I am speculating here, this is not a stretch of the imagination. Personally, speaking out against heresy, injustice, and racism both inside and outside the church has often resulted in strained, if not broken, relationships.

day soon, all we endure in this life will dissipate. Our suffering—whatever it might be—will be worth it all.

Jesus promises a portion of "hidden manna" as well as a white stone engraved with a new name to all who overcome.[25] Although promised to all, these rewards would have been particularly significant to believers in Pergamum. In comparison to parchment (for which Pergamum was well known), an engraved stone represents a message that is much more permanent. Similarly, the promise of hidden manna serves as an encouragement for those refusing to participate in pagan feasts and refuting false teaching that encouraged religious compromise. Both rewards speak directly to the pressures felt by the church in Pergamum. They also point toward eternal rewards for all believers and anticipate a future heavenly feast.

Manna (literally, "What is it?") refers to wafers of bread the Lord rained down on Israel each day as they wandered the desert for forty years.[26] The miraculous provision was both an act of grace, ensuring Israel's survival, and a test to see if they would trust the Lord and walk according to His instruction.[27] Manna served two purposes: one practical, one spiritual. It sustained Israel the entire time they were in the desert, and it foreshadowed the One who gives life to the world. "I am the bread of life," Jesus says, "he who comes to Me will not hunger, and he who believes in Me will never thirst." The promise of a portion of hidden manna indicates fellowship and identification with Christ, both eternally secured in heaven.[28]

---

25   Revelation 2:17.
26   Compare Exodus 16:15 in the NASB and KJV. The Hebrew word used here, *man* (mawn), translates as "Who?" or "What?"
27   Exodus 16:4.
28   Beale, *The Book of Revelation*, 252.

The wonder of this promise is that it introduces an "already/ not yet" tension. Certainly, Jesus's invitation to come to Him as the bread of life was immediate, and we can enjoy true satisfaction in this life only when we follow Him. Amidst the world's countless temptations for more, Christians can respond, "I have food to eat that you do not know about."[29] Yet, the satisfaction Christians experience now is only a foretaste of what's to come. When we leave this life for eternal life with Christ, we will no longer experience even the temptation to sin or compromise our faith. The woes we feel in this life will dissipate like steam on a warm day, replaced with peace and joy in the presence of our Lord. Tears will be a thing of the past. Pain will eventually be forgotten. Death itself will be defeated. What wondrous rewards await those who overcome the trials and temptations of life!

In ancient society, the white stone held many meanings, each of them significant to followers of Jesus. First, it indicated an acquittal in a court of law. When a council rendered their verdict, they did so with either a black stone (indicating guilt) or a white stone (indicating acquittal). John wrote that the Father judges no one, "but He has given all judgment to the Son."[30] Jesus giving believers a white stone indicates His judgment: not guilty. Even though we are guilty of sin (none of us can say we have lived a sinless life), Jesus promises a white stone if we overcome. Second, the white stone represented a seal of friendship shared between two people. They would break the stone in two, each person retaining one half. Much like the half-heart pendant jewelry shared between friends (BFFs) today, the white stone signifies a close, intimate relationship between the Son of God and the one who overcomes. Third, a white stone was given to victors at athletic games, granting them access to a feast restricted to invitation-only. Jesus personally invites

---

29   John 4:32.
30   John 5:22.

those who overcome to a private feast. John wrote about this feast in Revelation 19:9, when an angel told him to write, "Blessed are those who are invited to the marriage supper of the Lamb."

One day, each of us who overcome will receive a white stone from Jesus representing acquittal, a vibrant relationship with Him, and spiritual victory through the Son of God. That stone will grant us a seat at the table for the marriage supper of the Lamb. Oh! What a day that will be!

Revelation 2:18–29

18 *"And to the angel of the church in Thyatira write: The Son of God, who has eyes like a flame of fire, and His feet are like burnished bronze, says this:*

19 *'I know your deeds, and your love and faith and service and perseverance, and that your deeds of late are greater than at first.*

20 *'But I have this against you, that you tolerate the woman Jezebel, who calls herself a prophetess, and she teaches and leads My bond-servants astray so that they commit acts of immorality and eat things sacrificed to idols.*

21 *'I gave her time to repent, and she does not want to repent of her immorality.*

22 *'Behold, I will throw her on a bed of sickness, and those who commit adultery with her into great tribulation, unless they repent of her deeds.*

23 *'And I will kill her children with pestilence, and all the churches will know that I am He who searches the minds and hearts; and I will give to each one of you according to your deeds.*

24 *'But I say to you, the rest who are in Thyatira, who do not hold this teaching, who have not known the deep things of Satan, as they call them—I place no other burden on you.*

25 *' Nevertheless what you have, hold fast until I come.*

26 *'He who overcomes, and he who keeps My deeds until the end, to him i will give authority over the nations;*

27 *and he shall rule them with a rod of iron, as the vessels of the potter are broken to pieces, as I also have received authority from My Father;*

28 *and I will give him the morning star.*

29 *'He who has an ear, let him hear what the Spirit says to the churches.'*

Chapter 5
The Letter to Thyatira

O f the seven cities included in the Revelation letters, Thyatira was the smallest. The city was known for its artisan craftsman, specifically metalworking and fabrics. It specialized in manufacturing a purple dye that was more affordable than that produced by Phoenicia. Luke wrote of a woman named Lydia from Thyatira who sold purple fabrics receiving the gospel from Paul.[1] It is believed she brought the gospel back to her hometown, becoming an evangelist for Christ and hosting church meetings in her home.[2]

Being a city specializing in crafts, trade guilds dominated the culture. Artisans were required to be members of these guilds in order to practice their trade. Like modern-day labor unions, trade guilds trained apprentices and journeymen, ensuring craftsmen met certain standards before considering them a master of a particular trade. Each guild also had a patron deity who brought success or failure, depending on how pleased they were. Guild members were required to worship patron deities through ceremonial offerings and

---

1   Acts 16:14.
2   Cynthia Long Westfall, *Paul and Gender: Reclaiming the Apostle's Vision for Men and Women in Christ* (Grand Rapids, MI: Baker Academic, 2016), 267.

feasts. Refusing to participate might displease the patron deity and bring hardship to the guild. Refusal, then, put a person's livelihood at risk, since they could be expelled from the guild and forbidden to work in their craft. As we've learned in the previous chapters, this was one of many challenges every Christian found themselves in.

Churches responded differently to these various difficulties. The church in Thyatira seems to have adopted pagan practices and doctrine, actually folding them into the teachings of Christianity. Rather than resist the dominant culture, this church chose to become part of it. In response, Jesus sent one of the strongest rebukes contained in any of the Revelation letters.

No Such Thing as a Small Compromise

Jesus foreshadows the content of His letter by using language alluding to judgment, referring to His "eyes like a flame of fire" and "feet like burnished bronze."[3] In chapter one, we learned that fire and bronze symbolize purification and judgment. Describing His eyes as being like fire gestures toward Christ's penetrating gaze. Indeed, in verse twenty-three, Jesus tells the church that He "searches the minds and hearts" of people, seeing not only their deeds but what G. Campbell Morgan calls "the forces that lie behind their works."[4] Depending on how we are living, this is either comforting or terrifying. Jesus's unsettling introduction shakes the church in Thyatira awake, conveying the seriousness of their actions. The unbelieving citizens of Thyatira may have seen the church's willingness to compromise as progressive and affirming. Jesus, however, indicated that the church was flirting with spiritual death.

---

3   Revelation 2:18.
4   G. Campbell Morgan, *The Letters of Our Lord: A First Century Message to Twentieth Century Christians* (London, U.K.: Pickering and Inglis LTD), 57.

But not all was wrong in Thyatira. Before His rebuke, Jesus acknowledges their increasing acts of love for people. Jesus notes that He knows their deeds and the love, faith, service, and perseverance stimulating them. First-century Christians (including those in Thyatira) lived in a culture and society aligned against them: civic leaders promoted anti-Christian bias and persecution, while leaders of the various religions besmirched Christians for any number of reasons. Yet, with seemingly every institution actively against them, believers in Thyatira continued to pour themselves into the city, and their later deeds were actually greater than the first. Rather than abandon their initial acts of love and service (like Ephesus), Christians in Thyatira doubled down on them. Morgan writes the works in Thyatira were "not an accident" but "a habit."[5] There was a consistency to the work being done in Thyatira, and, when love and action resonate with each other, beautiful things happen.

How do we compare to the church in Thyatira? As Christians, how do we respond when laws are passed, people elected, or decisions made that we perceive as being "anti-Christian"? Do our acts of love increase? Do we respond to adversity by continuing to serve others with a heart of love? Or do we run to the nearest keyboard and start typing our opinions on social media?

Love *produces* service in the same way that faith *produces* endurance.[6] Love and faith are motivators, the engines driving acts of service for the Lord and the people in our sphere of influence. They maintain a steady perseverance, allowing us to keep our eyes focused on Jesus regardless of circumstances. In spite of a culture that marginalized them, Christians in Thyatira loved and served others well. Paradoxically, both acceptable deeds and heretical doctrine increased over time in the Thyatiran church. Jesus was

---

5   *ibid*, 58.
6   James 1:3 and 2 Peter 1:5-7.

pleased with their deeds toward others, but He was supremely displeased with their response to the persistent cultural pressure to conform. In the words of Warren Wiersbe, "No amount of loving and sacrificial works can compensate for tolerance of evil."[7]

Things are about to get intense.

Compromise Endangers Many

Jesus rebukes Thyatira for allowing a woman He calls Jezebel to continue teaching and leading His "bond-servants astray so that they commit acts of immortality and eat things sacrificed to idols."[8] The name of the woman in question was probably not Jezebel, but in referencing the Old Testament queen, Jesus gave a dire warning both to her and all who followed her. The historical record of 1 Kings describes Jezebel as the daughter of the king of Sidonia, a pagan nation who worshiped Baal and Ashtoreth. Ahab, the king of the northern kingdom of Israel, married Jezebel, usurping the Mosaic law forbidding intermarriage with pagan nations.[9] Like Thyatira's Jezebel, Queen Jezebel influenced Ahab and, by extension, the entire kingdom to set aside God's law and worship pagan deities. Jezebel herself ruled through fear, using murder and theft to her profit. Many in Israel bowed under her oppression, choosing survival over the myriad tortures she levied against her enemies.

Thyatira tolerated a woman teaching paganism as part of Christianity. She was, to them, a modern-day Jezebel endangering their standing with the Lord should they continue with her. To be sure, Jesus did not take issue with her gender, but her doctrine. She was exactly the type of teacher Peter warned against: "There will also be false teachers among you, who will secretly introduce destructive

---

7   Wiersbe, *The Bible Exposition Commentary*, 575.
8   Revelation 2:20.
9   Deuteronomy 7:3. This is not a law forbidding miscegenation, but religious syncretism.

heresies, even denying the Master who bought them, bringing swift destruction upon themselves."[10] She did not teach in the shadows or privately practice paganism, she is openly taught heresy, and the church tolerated it. Unlike the Ephesian church which could not "tolerate evil men," Thyatira allowed her to continue, and—like the Old Testament Jezebel—she brought the church to the brink of its own destruction.

The Jezebel in Thyatira called herself a prophetess (one who speaks for the Lord), but she led Jesus's disciples astray, promoting idolatry and immorality as Christian principles. These were the same teachings secretly accepted by members of the church in Pergamum and fiercely guarded against in Ephesus. New Testament scholar, Colin Hemer, asserts, "It is quite conceivable that in this racially mixed city [of Thyatira], the church was threatened by some monstrous syncretism of Christian, Jewish, and pagan elements through a priestess who combined 'magical Judaism' or gnostic views with a professed adherence to Christianity."[11] She combined pagan practices with Christianity and taught them as if they came directly from the Lord. And the church allowed it. This was more than mere compromise. She bent the teachings of Christ to her own will, and the church accepted it. It's no wonder Jesus responded so strongly.

The Thyatiran letter reminds us to remain vigilant against anything that pulls us away from Jesus—the Way, the Truth, and the Life. There have always been false prophets—people who say they speak for God but don't—and the Lord has consistently warned against them. John wrote, "Beloved, do not believe every spirit, but test the spirits to see whether they are from God, because many false prophets have gone out into the world."[12] If someone

---

10   2 Peter 2:1.
11   Hemer, *The Letters to the Seven Churches*, 117.
12   1 John 4:1.

claims to speak for God, what they say must always align with God's Word. The "gospel" Jezebel taught may have promised job retention and continued support for their families, but justification and acceptance of sin endangered the eternity of everyone who heard and embraced her teaching. Compromises to our faith are not only dangerous—they are also incredibly short-sighted. Sin is never satisfied. It devours and desires more in an endless, destructive cycle, eventually consuming the sinners themselves.

Compromise Refuses Grace

God's good news extends beyond this life, promising eternal life with Him. And yes, God's grace is amazing, but it does not nullify the sinfulness of sin, nor does it allow us to make God in our own image. Instead, the work of the Holy Spirit (by His grace) consistently changes us—"from glory to glory"—into the image of Christ.[13] It looks beyond our sinfulness to extend forgiveness, Christ's righteousness, and eternal life and hope to all who answer His invitation to daily take up their cross and follow Him. Jezebel's teaching in Thyatira was an abuse of God's grace couched in the gnostic/prophetic language of hidden truth and new revelation. Jesus reveals their source, calling them "the deep things of Satan."[14] Jezebel may have been a member of a church, but she was not a member of the body of Christ.

Compromising our faith—for any reason—is not Christ-like. We can't escape temptation (Jesus Himself was tempted), but Christ set us free from the power of sin. For as long as the Church has existed, culture has forced Christians to choose between affirming worldliness or standing on their faith in Jesus as the Son of God. Following Jesus may include suffering (see the chapter on Smyrna)

---

13   2 Corinthians 3:18.
14   Revelation 2:24.

but suffering is no reason to compromise our faith. Although we are "called unto liberty," we are not to use our liberty as permission to sin.[15] To the Corinthians, Paul echoed a popular refrain ("all things are lawful") to correct dangerous practices, arguing that all things are not "profitable," nor do they "edify," even if they are lawful.[16] Civil law has never been the standard of holiness. Jesus is. That's why His invitation has always been, "Follow Me."

The false prophet in Thyatira consistently refused Christ's personal call to repentance. "I gave her time to repent," Jesus says, "but she does not want to repent of her immorality."[17] Even after lying about speaking for God and leading Jesus's flock away from Him toward destruction, Jesus gave her time to repent. What grace! It reminds me of Peter's admonition: "The Lord is not slow about His promise [to return], as some count slowness, but is patient toward you, not wishing for any to perish but for all to come to repentance."[18] Jesus's love extended even to the Thyatiran Jezebel, but she wanted no part of it. Repentance—like everything in Christianity—is a choice. Jesus forces no one to follow Him. He only offers the opportunity to repent, to accept His sacrifice for sin, and embrace Him as both Lord and Savior. She refused Him, and her obstinacy would prove costly.

Jesus holds nothing back in His proclamation of punishment. First, He says, "I will throw her on a bed."[19] The power she proudly enjoys dissipates in a word: throw. She cannot resist Christ's power. She cannot annul His authority. He will throw her on a bed. The bed gestures to her own sinfulness and the sin with which she entices others. The Greek word *porneuo* (porn-**yoo**-oh) is translated as

---

15 Galatians 5:13, KJV.
16 1 Corinthians 10:23.
17 Revelation 2:21.
18 2 Peter 3:9.
19 Revelation 2:22.

"immorality" in the New American Standard Bible and "fornication" in the King James. *Porneuo* is sexual immorality, and the use of the word in Jesus's admonishment of Jezebel's teaching drives home a simple yet powerful principle: idolatry (in any form) is spiritual adultery. Jesus sees it as His bride exchanging His eternal promise for momentary pleasure. Even so, the offer of repentance persists. Judgment has been promised, but until it is meted out, anyone can confess their sin and live a life of repentance. But only if they want to.

Pride Comes Before Destruction

The rebuke recorded in this letter is both the longest and the most strongly worded. Christ's language is specific, suggesting particularity. He speaks of the Thyatiran Jezebel in a way that suggests everyone knew who she was and what she taught. (I often wonder if she was in attendance when the letter was read to the congregation. Oh, to be a fly on the wall that day!) While punishment, suffering, and death dominate this section of the letter, the notion of escape repeatedly surfaces throughout. The suffering Jesus describes is avoidable if one will only humble themselves and repent, choosing fidelity to Christ over self-preservation.

The tribulation referred to in verse twenty-two gestures toward the years of "great tribulation" chronicled in the middle chapters of Revelation. During that time, sinners suffer and die horrific deaths. Ironically, in seeking to escape suffering at the hands of society and the state, the false prophet in Thyatira and her "children" suffer instead at the hands of God.

Calling followers of the Thyatiran Jezebel her "children" carries significant weight, indicating their true spiritual status in the kingdom of God. While speaking to a Jewish ruler, Jesus said,

"Unless one is born again, he cannot see the kingdom of God."[20] Jesus drew a distinction between a person's physical birth and their spiritual birth. Indeed, all religious conversion is a spiritual birth of some sort. However, Christ argues that unless a person is "born of the Spirit," they "cannot enter the kingdom of God."[21] The disciples of the false teacher in Thyatira were spiritual children—they had been born into a religious doctrine—but the spirit by which they were born was not the Holy Spirit. Therefore, although they may have been members of a Christ-following church, they were not members of the body of Christ—a dangerous position, indeed.

It is better to be broken and healed by Jesus than to ignore Him and be destroyed. Matthew records Jesus saying, "He who falls on this stone [Himself] will be broken to pieces; but on whomever it falls, it will scatter him like the dust."[22] Jesus declares to Thyatira that those who refuse Him won't just die, He will "kill them with pestilence [death]."[23] They would die in a manner that was unmistakably from the Lord. It's the same fate as that of the Old Testament Queen Jezebel and her seventy sons. When they died, everyone knew it was the Lord who brought it to pass. Similarly, when fire and brimstone leveled Sodom, Gomorrah, and surrounding cities, nobody questioned from Whom such destruction came; when the walls of Jericho fell flat at the shout of God's people, everyone knew Who caused such a miraculous (albeit horrifying) event. When God acts, there is no doubt. Jesus's feet are shod with burnished bronze—judgment is coming, and "all the churches will know that I am He who searches the minds and hearts."[24]

---

20   John 3:3.
21   John 3:5-6.
22   Matthew 21:44.
23   Revelation 2:23.
24   Revelation 2:23.

It's important to restate that Jesus's complaint against the church itself is their silence and tolerance of Jezebel's teaching and influence, while reserving His stern warning and punishment for those living in sinful error. Paradoxically, it is possible for love and good works to increase in the same church that doctrinal heresy is being taught. Obviously, this is not ideal, and I am in no way suggesting heresy should be allowed to continue in any church purporting to follow Jesus. The implication of the letter is that the church should do all it can to oppose false teaching. However, Jesus puts only one burden on the faithful of the church in Thyatira: hold fast.

Resisting Winds of Change

Steadfastness, endurance, and perseverance are common themes throughout the New Testament. Describing the last days, Jesus says, "because lawlessness is increased, most people's love will grow cold. But the one who endures to the end, he will be saved."[25] New Testament authors all firmly believed Jesus's return was imminent and the reward of heaven was near. To them, Christ's description of the last days seemed increasingly evident: lawlessness increased, and love grew colder. Jesus had not been gone for a full generation before heresy, idolatry, and immorality became folded into His teaching. However, Jesus's letter indicates many in Thyatira resisted false doctrine. Jesus exhorts them with a simple message: "What you have, hold fast until I come."

What did the faithful in Thyatira have? We could say they had good works, acts of service which Jesus approved of and wanted to continue. However, the motivation for works can change over time, especially when the surrounding culture becomes more challenging.

---

25   Matthew 24:12-13.

Look at Ephesus, whose defense of the gospel transformed into a loveless legalism, pushing people away from Christ rather than drawing them in. The reason for our work is as important as the work itself. Certainly, Jesus wanted Thyatira to continue in their good works. But more importantly, Jesus wanted them to hold fast to the *why* behind their good works: their love for, and faith in, Jesus Christ.

As the world becomes more sinful and love grows colder, Christianity runs the risk of devolving into a defined set of religious activities, making it easier for people to *act* like Christians without actually *being* Christ-like. This is why love is so vital. Jesus taught that the greatest commandment in all Scripture is love: love for God and love for people. Love is a foundational principle, promoting faith in God, willingness to serve others, and perseverance in times of hardship. In a culture promoting constant grabbing and getting, Christians pursue love from the core of their being. Friend, as the world changes around us, let's hold fast to our love for God and people. Let's love God with all we are and have; and let's love others like ourselves. That sort of love will shine as a beacon in an ever-darkening world.

What did the believers in Thyatira have? They had the gospel—the true gospel, the "power of God for salvation to everyone who believes."[26] It needs no other validation than that which has already been given: the cross and the empty tomb. The gospel is self-sufficient, needing no additional "deep thing" to make it more effective, no new revelation to make it clearer. Jesus died for our sins, and He rose from the dead, taking captivity captive and giving us hope for eternal life with Him. In spite of the shifting sands of culture and the Church's own sordid history, the gospel remains

---

26 Romans 1:16.

unchanged.[27] Jesus is still the Son of God; His sacrifice is still enough; His tomb is still empty; His grace is still sufficient for us.

"What you have hold fast until I come." Hold fast to the love of God and to the gospel, to the grace and hope conveyed in the Good News of Jesus. Its relevance extends into all cultures because people need a Savior regardless of where or when they live. Reject any message that does not align with the gospel. Mark it as false and dangerous. Morgan explains, "The message [Christ] has delivered is complete, the doctrine is enunciated, the mysteries are revealed, and whomsoever, man or woman, would claim to reveal a new mystery, is the messenger of Satan"[28] Strong words, yet necessary because eternity is at stake. Jesus gives no other burden to the faithful in Thyatira but the burden of His gospel. Hold fast to the gospel of Christ and carry it to the world.

Jesus is Coming

Jesus's counsel is also His promise: "hold fast until I come." Jesus *is* coming back. The message of His return recurs throughout the New Testament, and has energized believers from the very beginning of the Church until today. Here is just a small sampling of verses containing the promise of Jesus's return:

- Jesus told His disciples, "If I go and prepare a place for you, I will come again and receive you to Myself."[29]
- An angel exhorted the disciples, saying, "This Jesus, who has been taken up from you into heaven, will come in just the same way as you have watched..."[30]

---

27   To be sure, the Church is responsible for several wonderful contributions: innovating hospitals and promoting the expansion of universities. However, the Church is also responsible for unspeakable horrors, including death and destruction wrought against people in the name of Jesus. Nevertheless, the Gospel remains unchanged regardless of man's influence on the Church throughout history.

28   Morgan, *Letters*, 65.

29   John 14:3.

30   Acts 1:11.

- Paul wrote, "For the Lord Himself will descend from heaven with a shout, with the voice of the archangel and with the trumpet of God..."[31]
- Three times in the last chapter of Revelation, Jesus says, "Behold, I am coming quickly."

We may not know *when* He will return (many have attempted to figure this out), but the date is not the point. Jesus did not encourage Thyatira to "hold fast until I come" hoping they would spend time, energy, and resources calculating the exact date of His coming. It's not for us "to know the times or epoch which the Father has fixed by His own authority."[32] Instead, Jesus wants us concerned with preaching the gospel, baptizing believers, and making disciples. You know, the Great Commission. He wants His disciples finding comfort in *knowing* He is returning. For centuries, Jesus's impending return encouraged believers to hold on to their faith under the harshest of circumstances.

Quick question: if you knew Jesus was coming tomorrow, what would you be able or willing to endure today?

Waiting for anything gets frustrating over time, especially when day after day of waiting is filled with hardship. The empty promises of compromise only make waiting that much harder. Significantly, all Jesus had for Thyatira was the promise of His return; but that was all they needed. His promise is all we need. Holding on to that promise, allowing it (not our circumstances) to motivate our lives, is a choice, one with the divine potential to shape all aspects of our lives. Peter says the day of Jesus's return will "come like a thief," unexpected and without warning. The truth is we don't know when He's coming. It may not be today or tomorrow or even next year, but He *is* coming. "Behold, I'm coming quickly," Jesus says, "and

---

31   1 Thessalonians 4:16.
32   Acts 1:7-8.

my reward is with Me."[33] Jesus promises He will return, and He hasn't failed on a promise yet. Don't lose heart. Jesus is coming soon!

Jesus Is Who He Says He Is

Verses twenty-six through twenty-eight of chapter two contain another of Jesus's promises for those who overcome. In it, Jesus indicates a reversal of the power structure experienced in the first century Greco-Roman world. Those exploiting and oppressing others will, one day, find themselves subjugated under Christ's authority which He delegates to His followers. The vision John records later in Revelation seems to confirm this: "Then I saw thrones, and they sat on them, and judgment was given to them."[34] Through this interpretive lens, the letter—indeed, all of Revelation—reads like an anti-Roman manifesto in coded language. The Roman Empire is temporary; Christ's kingdom is forever, and one day the same Christians being persecuted will rule with a rod of iron. Encouraging? Yes. But this promise is so much more!

Jesus is not using coded language, He is using rabbinical language; and He is not merely describing a transfer of power, but confirming who He is so that those suffering in His name can find solace. Rabbis rarely answered a question posed by their disciples directly. Instead, they asked a leading question or quoted a single line from the Bible, encouraging their students to really think, while at the same time pointing them in the direction of the answer. In the New Testament, we see Jesus often doing the same thing with His disciples. For example, while imprisoned, John the Baptist sent messengers to Jesus asking, "Are you the expected One, or do we look for someone else?"[35] Jesus sent them back to report

---

33   Revelation 22:12.
34   Revelation 20:4.
35   Luke 7:19.

what they saw: "the blind receive sight, the lame walk, the lepers are cleansed, and the deaf hear, the dead are raised up, the poor have the gospel preached to them."[36] He could have simply said, "Yes." Instead, His non-reply reply led John to Messianic prophecies, confirming what John already knew: Jesus is the Messiah.

In the same way, Jesus refers to messianic texts in this promise to overcomers in which He paraphrases the second Psalm:

> *Ask of Me, and I will surely give the nations as Your inheritance, and the very ends of the earth as Your possession. You shall break them with a rod of iron, You shall shatter them like earthenware.*[37]

According to Grant Osborn, first-century Jews interpreted this psalm as messianic, foreshadowing the time when the Lord's anointed, His Christ, would establish His rule on the earth.[38] He is, in fact, the promised Messiah, and no government, no emperor, no iteration of culture can ever change that fact. Jesus owns the nations and the earth. He possesses the rod of iron and all authority. According to His promise to Thyatira, He will one day grant both His authority and power to His followers, a source of hope for all those struggling under oppressive powers in place over them. It indicates an utter reversal of power if they will just hold on to their faith in Him.

The final gift in the letter is the most precious: the morning star. Within the last recorded message of Jesus in Scripture, Christ describes Himself as "the root and descendant of David, the *bright morning star*."[39] Jesus is the morning star. He is our great (and greatest) reward. Life as a Christian includes hardship and struggle and spiritual battles, but Christ has already won the victory.

---

36   Luke 7:22.
37   Psalm 2:8-9.
38   Osborne, *Revelation*, 165.
39   Revelation 22:16.

Following Jesus always carries a cost. Indeed, it costs us our lives. Paul expressed this beautifully, writing, "I have been crucified with Christ; and it is no longer I who live, but Christ lives in me."[40] Regardless of the cost, this final promise reminds us that what we will gain in the next life will be so much more than anything we lose in this life.

The truth is, the world will always be offended by Jesus. Admittedly, the Church has erred badly throughout history, leaving trauma and pain in its wake. However, even if Christians lived in perfect faith, we would still offend people who don't know Him. Jesus Himself (who we can all agree lived in perfect accord to the Great Commandment) offended many; and the political, social, and religious communities combined forces to crucify the Son of God. However, we can't allow the fear of being canceled cause us to compromise our faith to appease others.

Does this mean we resist our culture by ignoring everyone who isn't a Christian, sheltering ourselves from the "outside" world? No. Should we shout down other peoples' opinions and impose our own religious beliefs on them? Absolutely not! Instead, we intentionally pursue Jesus, and resist the worldly demand to adopt opinions and ideologies that are far from Christ. And we *definitely* don't try to spin those ideologies to fit some sort of Christian framework, justifying attitudes and lifestyles that are not Christ-like. Like Jesus, we treat everyone (regardless of their faith) with the love and dignity they deserve as human beings and image bearers of God. We gracefully preach the gospel, while faithfully living out the gospel ourselves. Christianity is not a private faith. It is a personal faith, lived publicly.

---

40   Galatians 2:20.

Endure unto the end.

Hold fast until He comes.

He is coming soon.

Revelation 3:1–6

1   *"To the angel of the church in Sardis write: He who has the seven Spirits of God and the seven stars, says this: 'I know your deeds, that you have a name that you are alive, but you are dead.*

2   *'Wake up, and strengthen the things that remain, which were about to die; for I have not found your deeds completed in the sight of My God.*

3   *'So remember what you have received and heard; and keep it, and repent. Therefore if you do not wake up, I will come like a thief, and you will not know at what hour I will come to you.*

4   *'But you have a few people in Sardis who have not soiled their garments; and they will walk with Me in white, for they are worthy.*

5   *'He who overcomes will thus be clothed in white garments; and I will not erase his name from the book of life, and I will confess his name before My Father and before His angels.*

6   *'He who has an ear, let him hear what the Spirit says to the churches.'*

Chapter 6

The Letter to Sardis

Congratulations! You've gone beyond the halfway point of the book. There's no going back now. There has been a *lot* of information thrown at you so far, so perhaps now is a good time to pause and review.

The churches in Asia Minor each faced similar spiritual pressures. Between the imperial cult and the worship of patron deities in trade guilds, paganism had become ingrained as part of the cultural identity. Refusal to participate meant social ostracism at best. For many, it meant the loss of one's ability to work. Other possibilities included exile, the loss of all one's possessions, and—in extreme cases—execution. Christians daily felt pressured to soften their stance on sin and their belief in one God and one mediator between God and man, namely Jesus Christ.

If I were to categorize the letters, the first four would fall under the category of responding to pressure to compromise on doctrine. Churches weathered continual bombardments of doctrines peddling compromise as the solution to hardship. Church leaders struggled with the constant tension between watching their congregations suffer and promoting religious syncretism to relieve their suffering. Ephesus responded to false teaching by militantly rejecting it; Smyrna suffered for refusing to compromise; Pergamum turned a blind eye to members of their church adopting certain pagan practices; and Thyatira adopted compromise as Christian practice.

The rest of the letters address the temptation for churches (and church leaders) to conform to worldly standards. Beginning with Sardis, we will see how they dealt with the disparity between the culture of the Kingdom of God and of the dominant culture in which they lived.

Sardis—the capital of the ancient Lydian kingdom—was situated against steep cliffs, making it an almost impregnable military stronghold. It was a good thing, since gold and silver were the primary commodities of the kingdom. Legend had it that Midas left his golden touch behind in the spring that ran through the city. Fun fact: under its second king, Croesus (pronounced: **cree**-sus), Lydia was the first kingdom to use minted coins as currency. Where do you think those coins were minted? Yep, Sardis. The wealth of Lydia was so well known, that the phrase "rich as Croesus" became a common idiom in the surrounding regions.

Pride goes before a fall, though, and King Cyrus of Persia captured Sardis in 546 BCE after only fourteen days of a siege. How was this unimaginable feat accomplished? One of his soldiers scaled an unwatched portion of the surrounding cliffs, crept into the city, and opened the gates. As improbable an act as that was, it was repeated centuries later. This time, by Cretan soldiers climbing yet another unwatched section of the cliff while the city guard watched the main road. Twice the city fell due to lapses in judgment from the watchmen entrusted with the city's safety. Twice the enemy exploited what the city considered to be their strongest defense: the cliffs. Trust in natural defenses and their exceedingly great resources led the people of Sardis to grow complacent. That complacency led directly to their downfall. Twice.

In the late first century, the church in Sardis seemed to be walking down the same path as its home city. Jesus's letter to them is a warning: they path they are now on leads to the same result.

It's a Matter of Trust

The letter suggests the church had chosen the path of least resistance in response to the surrounding culture, making no real effort to resist persistent paganism or to preach the gospel in an effective way. Instead, they seemed content to simply exist, mind their own business, and survive. Rather than compromise, the church in Sardis decided it was much easier to maintain a low profile and remain invisible. The church existed, but Jesus warns that merely existing is not living, suggesting they were repeating the mistake made by Sardis centuries earlier: believing they were safe when in fact they were in mortal danger.

To the church doing everything in its power to escape persecution and survive, Jesus identifies Himself as the One who is the power of the Church. The "seven spirits of God" are not seven literal spirits.[1] Like the seven lampstands, term is symbolic, representing the fullness of God's power and authority. Paul described Jesus to the Colossians as "the fullness of deity" dwelling "in bodily form."[2] The image implies that the power Jesus possesses is far greater than the power any government can wield over a local church, or that a church can wield in its own protection.

Jesus also holds the seven stars ("angels" of the churches),

---

1   Revelation 3:1.
2   Colossians 2:9.

reminding Sardis that He is in control, and anything they need is contained in Him alone. When the proverbial wheels come off the bus, we can always turn to Jesus, who is faithful to give out of His fullness.[3] Jesus Himself is the power of and provider for the church. He is also its ministry and message. The introduction presents a powerful image, reminding Sardis that Christ's people must learn to trust Him when trials come—and they will come.

How easily we tend to forget that.

The modern-day church in America has a relevance problem. A recent study conducted by the Pew Research Center indicates a steady decline of people identifying as Christian, with a corresponding increase of people claiming no religious affiliation at all (a group labeled "nones").[4] The report estimates that Christians will no longer be in the majority in America by 2070. Although the report is new, the trend away from Christianity is not. For decades, churches have collaborated to create movements to draw people into (or back into) the fold. Each iteration of those movements contained the rallying cry of relevance. A few decades ago, this played out as churches crafting environments that were familiar to people outside the church (think movie theaters, clubs, concert halls, etc.), and preachers presenting a message that was more palatable to "outsiders." I know because I rode that same wave, attended the same church leadership conferences, had the same discussions in church, and made similar changes to my own messaging. Looking back (or, more correctly, looking in), it seems we fell into the trap of believing familiarity would result in life change. That people far from God would be drawn to our churches because they looked and sounded like spaces they already inhabited. Were there positive

---

3   John 1:16.
4   "Modeling the Future of Religion in America," *Pew Research Center,* September 13, 2022. https://www.pewresearch.org/religion/2022/09/13/modeling-the-future-of-religion-in-america/

results from this movement? Absolutely, but they were limited in scope. Tragically, the more common result has been churches that are all but invisible, preaching around the gospel rather than the gospel itself.

Like Sardis, somewhere along the line we forgot that Jesus is everything to and for the church. We've given in to our darker natures and (re)created Jesus in our own image, believing He thinks like us, acts like us, and votes like us. We've forgotten that Jesus is neither a member of a political party, nor is He an American citizen. We've avoided the implications of the fact that God created a world without borders. Any conflation of political platforms and/or patriotism with Christianity and the gospel is the exact thing Jesus spoke *against* in these seven letters. Jesus alone has the seven spirits of God. He alone holds the seven stars. He alone determines the outcomes of our efforts. When we depend on our abilities and strategies to survive or to reach people, we have given up on the very thing we have to offer them, namely Jesus.

With few exceptions, the church in Sardis believed they controlled their destiny. They may have accomplished meaningful works in their past, but when the cultural environment heated up, they considered the safest road one of silent, private faith. Christian faith is not private. It's personal. In this letter, Jesus firmly exhorts His people to come out from behind closed doors and do something. Come what may.

Lulled to Sleep

The backhanded compliment to Sardis ("You have a name that you're alive") suggests they aren't really alive but dead. They had a *name* that they were alive. They built a reputation with people outside of Christianity who saw them as spiritual people, thriving in the city one way or another. In reality, though, they were spiritually dying. Their previous works may have established them as a spiritually-thriving church, but there were now no longer any signs of spiritual life. What happened?

Significantly, the letter gives no indication of doctrinal issues like in Thyatira and Pergamos, nor do they seem to suffer persecution like the Smyrnaean church. There simply aren't any pressures (culturally, doctrinally, or politically) being felt by the church. Warren Wiersbe addresses this phenomenon when he writes, "No friction usually means no motion! The unsaved in Sardis saw the church as a respectable group of people who were neither dangerous nor desirable. They were decent people with a dying witness and a decaying ministry."[5] Although they existed in the midst of the city, they no longer had an influence in the city. They had grown invisible and unfelt like lukewarm water (more on this in the chapter on Laodicea).

The church in Sardis repeated the mistakes the city's guardians made centuries earlier. They grew lax in watching over themselves, believing they had done enough already to protect from harm. They trusted in their ability to control their destiny, believing their enemy to be political or cultural forces. They forgot that their real enemy (Satan) is not a people at all, and that he is a master deceiver who has nothing but time to find and exploit our weaknesses. All he did for Sardis was wait, and in a relatively short time, the church grew complacent and slowly (ever so slowly) they began dying spiritually. This is a most dangerous place to be: fully believing you are spiritually thriving, yet actually on the precipice of spiritual death. Jesus's statement must have come as a shock. But that shock was exactly what the church needed (needs) to experience revival.

---

5   Wiersbe, *The Bible Exposition Commentary*, 577.

Waking up is the first step to any revival. The church in Sardis had begun going through the motions of Christianity. Have you ever been like that? Going to church but your heart's not in it; the songs are nice, but you're not "feeling it"; the sermons are good, but you don't engage with them; you feel no inclination to pray, no conviction to seek the Lord. You go to church every week, and you leave unchanged. Ephesus's heart might have been engaged for the wrong reasons, but the heart in Sardis wasn't engaged at all. Maybe the first step of revival is realizing we're asleep. Jesus's counsel was not given gently, nor is it a suggestion: "Wake up!"

Sardis had works, but they were incomplete in the sight of God. Those works may have satisfied the church in Sardis, they may have even satisfied the people of Sardis, but they did not satisfy Christ. Let's consider their works for a moment. There's no way of knowing exactly what they were doing, but we can make some assumptions: they probably gathered regularly for fellowship, teaching, and breaking bread together; and they may have shared communion and baptized the occasional new believer. Nothing seems wrong so far, right? Who wouldn't want to be a part of a church like that? But what if their works were only accomplished in a building? What if they only drew near to Christ when other believers were watching, but refused to follow Him completely? What if, by declaring their works incomplete, Christ was suggesting their Christianity extended only as far as the church home, and *those* works were treated more like a religious duty, void of love or compassion? Their sacrifice of praise was blemished, imperfect, incomplete. They looked like a church, but lacked the vivacity of Christ's Church. They had "a form of godliness" but denied "the power thereof."[6]

That was then. This is now. What if *we* are doing these same

---

6   2 Timothy 3:1.

things? What if we have compartmentalized our Christianity to exist within church buildings when it should permeate our lives? What if we have made Jesus a part of our lives rather than the center of our lives? Have we, like Sardis before us, fallen asleep? Are we spiritually dying but think we're thriving? Do we need to wake up?

While there is still breath in our lungs, there is hope for spiritual revitalization. My desperate prayer is for the Lord to use this book as a sort of wake-up call to all who may need it, challenging us to an honest, Holy Spirit-led self-examination to determine if we, too, have been derelict in our duty as watchmen. O Lord, shake us awake!

The rest of Jesus's counsel sounds like that which He gave to Ephesus. Ephesus had left their first love, so Jesus told them to remember and repent, doing their first works. Jesus directs Sardis (whose works are incomplete) to remember and repent, doing the things they initially received and heard. That pattern is not insignificant, for it is the pattern of revival: wake up, remember, and repent.

Sardis was on the brink of spiritual death, but it was not dead yet. Their lampstand remained and Jesus gave them the prescription for revival. On this side of heaven, no church—indeed, no person—is outside of Christ's ability to save. There is hope for a spiritually dead or dying church for the same reason there is hope for the spiritually dead or dying Christian: Christ brings new life. He offered to Sardis what He offers to all of us: Himself, the One with the seven spirits of God. If Sardis was to be truly revived, it needed the Father, the Son, and the Holy Spirit. If we want to be truly spiritually alive, we need the same. Without Him, we are just rattling bones.

God's Exceedingly Great Army

For me, the most powerful image depicting true spiritual revival is the vision Ezekiel had of the valley filled with dry bones.[7] The Lord never explains why those bones filled the valley or why there were so many of them in the first place. No cause of death is ever given, only that the bones were "very dry." Ezekiel had no power to do anything for these bones but see them and describe them.

But the Lord was about to speak life into them.

Even bones long baked in the desert sun can rejoin, reform, and come alive by the power of His Word. When Ezekiel speaks God's message to them ("O dry bones, hear the word of the Lord!"), he describes a "noise" and a "rattling" as bones came together, each to the ones to whom they belonged. After the great commotion, Ezekiel records that a great number of people stood in the valley, "but there was no breath in them." The valley had been filled with activity, and motion, and noise, but there was no life.

After being dry bones for so long, it would be easy to lean into the miracle of being formed (or reformed) into flesh and blood. *Look at us! We're not what we used to be!* Seriously, being a lifeless body is a step up from being very dry bones, right? Yet, as amazing as reformation is, they were all missing something—or should I say some One. They needed the Holy Spirit. God told Ezekiel to speak to the breath to breathe on them, so those who stood lifeless could "come to life."[8] The word translated "breath" in verse nine is the Hebrew word *ruwach* (**roo**-akh). That same word is translated "Spirit of God" in Genesis 1:2. Throughout the Bible, breath or wind signifies the invisible yet effectual power of the Holy Spirit. When the Holy Spirit entered those lifeless soldiers in the valley,

---

7   See Ezekiel 37.
8   Ezekiel 37:9.

they indeed came to life and stood together as "an exceedingly great army." It's one thing to gather as believers. It's another thing to perform religious liturgy or ceremony or service, to have activity and noise together as believers. It's an entirely different thing to be revived and empowered by the Holy Spirit.

The Holy Spirit empowers the Church to fulfill her mission of preaching the gospel with both their lives and their words. He encourages the Church when she faces persecution, and leads the Church to love the world and *be* the Church to the world. Comfort lulled Sardian believers into spiritual apathy, a powerless Christian experience marked by activity but no force. They had become all but invisible to the city. Their light: diminished. Their saltiness: bland. The Sardians needed the Holy Spirit.

Friend, *we* need the Holy Spirit. We need the Lord to speak life into us. We need the *ruwach* of God moving through us like air moving through our lungs. Only then will the Church's activity become unblemished worship that brings glory to the King of Kings. Only then will believers represent the Kingdom of God, a Kingdom without borders, a city on a hill which cannot be hidden. Only then will the Church be transformed from a pile of rattling bones into an exceedingly great army, an army that even the powers of Hades cannot defeat.[9]

Although the church in Sardis slipped into a spiritual coma, Christ assures them they are not yet lost. Wake up, He exhorts them, and strengthen what remains. Osborn writes, "This process of dying had been going on for some time and the culmination (their death) was right around the corner. They had to act quickly or die."[10] Waking up was the first step, to be immediately followed by

---

9   "...upon this rock I will build My Church; and the gates of Hades will not overpower it," Matthew 16:18.

10   Osborn, *Revelation*, 173.

strengthening what remained. Although the church as a whole was dead, there were remnants within it that could be strengthened—people that could be restored, attitudes that could be reinforced, activities that could be repeated. Christ encourages Sardis to remember what they had received and heard, and to start actually doing those things. That's repentance.

Jesus did not give up on Sardis (or any of the churches). He has not given up on you. If the Lord has found you sleeping, let this be a clarion call to you as well: wake up, remember, and repent.

Jesus's Return Means Victory

When Jesus spoke of His return to the church in Pergamum, He said, "I am coming quickly." To the Sardian church, He says, "I will come like a thief." Both indicate the suddenness and unexpectedness of His return. Not only by the world—those outside the Church—but by Christians as well, people who should—like watchmen—be looking for His return every day. For Sardis, the thief analogy would have been particularly meaningful, since their history recounts their sudden downfall (twice!) due to an unseen enemy sneaking into the city. Indeed, watchfulness was a common theme of Jesus's teaching to His followers. "Be ready," Jesus says, "for the Son of Man is coming at an hour that you do not expect."[11] By the time Jesus gave John this revelation, the Church had been enduring persecution, exile, and death for decades. It would have been easy to give up, to stop watching for Jesus's return, to stop even *believing* He was coming back. It's now almost two thousand years later and we're still waiting. Jesus ends the debate. He is coming back. Time passes, cultures change, kingdoms come and go, but Jesus's promise remains:

---

11   Luke 12:40.

> *Do not let your heart be troubled; believe in God, believe also in Me. In my Father's house are many dwelling places; if it were not so, I would have told you; for I go to prepare a place for you. If I go and prepare a place for you, I will come again and receive you to Myself, that where I am, there you may be also.*[12]

Rest assured: Jesus is coming soon, and His return means victory.

Garments are an important metaphor in Scripture, often referring to a person's spiritual life. "Let your priests be clothed with righteousness," the psalmist wrote.[13] Paul exhorted the Ephesians to "put off the old self," the self that practiced sin and embraced sinfulness, and "put on the new self...created in righteousness and holiness of the truth."[14] There were some in Sardis who had not "soiled their garments," who had not given in to the temptation to conform, who had remained steadfast in their personal (not private) faith in Jesus as the Son of God.[15] They had put on the "new man" and suffered the consequences. Many in the region had already lost their lives or livelihood because of it. Some viewed their demise as defeat. Jesus says otherwise. He calls them worthy. Beale notes that it is precisely because of their suffering that Jesus considers them worthy. They were "willing to follow the model of Jesus," who Himself suffered "on account of His faithful testimony."[16] The faith of some Sardian believers kept them from prestige, power, or wealth in this world, but Jesus assures them they walk with Him in the next, wearing white garments.

White garments signify the victory won by Christ and shared by His followers. When a Roman general won a monumental campaign, they were often rewarded with a Roman triumph, a parade through Rome celebrating their victory. The general and

---

12   John 14:1-3.
13   Psalms 132:9.
14   Ephesians 4:22-24.
15   Revelation 3:4.
16   Beale, *The Book of Revelation*, 276.

his army wore white as they rode and marched through the city, chained prisoners and spoils of war in tow. Jesus's resurrection indicates His triumph over all powers and principalities, granting us victory over sin and death. "O death, where is your victory," taunts Paul, "O death, where is your sting?"[17] By promising the church in Sardis they would be clothed in white garments, Jesus indicates they would be participants in His future triumphal parade. It's difficult—if not impossible—to overstate the impact this would have made on Sardian believers. Grant notes that defeat imprinted itself upon the cultural DNA of a city living in the "bitter memory of past triumph" and a history of resounding defeats.[18] Defeat became their identity, so passivity became their activity. If we don't try, we can't fail. Jesus's promise stands as incentive: to trust Him, to follow Him, to be salt and light—indeed, the Church—in the world. The world may never acknowledge our efforts, but we will celebrate Jesus's victory with Him very soon.

Jesus makes two promises regarding the names of those who overcome, who choose not to be "conformed to this world, but… transformed by the renewing of [their] mind."[19] The first is that He will not erase their name from the book of life. Not only is there a literal book, but the image draws on people's understanding of literal citizen registries that were common at the time. For example, Jews had a national registry because heritage held incredible power since family records dictated landownership. Matthew and Luke's Gospels both begin with the family ancestry leading to Jesus, revealing Him as both the Son of Man and the Son of God, the ultimate fulfillment of the Lord's promise to Abraham.[20] Grant notes that pagan nations also kept such records, asserting that Sardis, as the Lydian capital as well as a prominent city of both the Seleucid and

---

17 1 Corinthians 15:55.
18 Osborne, *Revelation*, 179.
19 Romans 12:2.
20 "In you, all the families of the earth will be blessed," Genesis 12:3.

Persian empires, may have been a repository for them.[21] Romans also kept civil rolls, since Roman citizenship came with many privileges. Those who received banishment or exile had their names stricken from these records, and all rights and privileges of citizenship were lost. The Sardian audience would have been intimately aware of the significance of Jesus's promise to not erase their names from the book of life. So, what *is* the book of life?

I'm glad you asked.

Revelation is not the only place we find references to the book of life. In Exodus, Moses pleads for Israel, petitioning God to instead "blot me out from Your book which You have written."[22] David wrote a psalm requesting that his enemies "be blotted out of the book of life" and "not recorded with the righteous."[23] The book of Daniel talks about a great time of distress from which those "found written in the book will be rescued."[24] Lastly (for the sake of time), Paul wrote of companions "whose names," he is sure, "are in the book of life."[25] OK, so the book of life is found throughout Scripture, but what, exactly, is it?

John answers that question toward the end of Revelation when he records the judgment of the dead gathered around Christ's great white throne. "If anyone's name was not found written in the book of life," John writes, "he was thrown into the lake of fire."[26] Simply put, we want our names in this book, and Jesus promises that every person who overcomes will not have their names erased from the book. "In this world you will have tribulation," Jesus assured His disciples, "but take courage; I have overcome the world."[27] Trusting

---

21   Osborne, *Revelation*, 180.
22   Exodus 32:32.
23   Psalm 69:28.
24   Daniel 12:1.
25   Philippians 4:3.
26   Revelation 20:15.
27   John 16:33.

Jesus is the pathway to overcoming; He is the only way to eternal life. Continue following Him and He promises your name will never be removed from His Book of Life.

Jesus also promises that He will confess those names before the Lord and His angels. This confession fulfills Christ's promise: "Whoever confesses me before men," He says, "I will also confess him before My Father."[28] The alternative to confessing Christ is to deny Him, to be ashamed of being associated with Him. This is where Sardis found themselves. Seeking to avoid conflict they denied their "Christian distinctives," disappearing into the crowd.[29] They still met as a church. They still prayed and worshiped God while gathered. They still believed the gospel message, but self-preservation led them to deny the power of gospel, what Paul called "the power of God unto salvation."[30] Jesus's promise was also a call to action. Confess Christ in this life, and He will confess you in the next.

There is a cost to confessing the Lordship of Jesus, a cost to following Him and walking His straight and narrow path toward eternal life. For Sardis (and perhaps for us as well), it meant the end of a comfortable, non-confrontational existence. It meant embracing the call to be separate from the world, different from those who do not know Jesus themselves. Jesus calls His disciples to this life *knowing* what it will cost. He wants us to choose His life in spite of the cost. He encourages us to lift our eyes from what we might lose by following Him, and instead focus on what Jesus guarantees is waiting for all who overcome. Whatever the cost might be for following Jesus, the reward will be far greater.

---

28   Matthew 10:32.
29   Osborne, *Revelation*, 180.
30   Romans 1:16.

Revelation 3:7–13

7 *"And to the angel of the church in Philadelphia write: He who is holy, who is true, who has the key of David, who opens and no one will shut, and who shuts and no one opens, says this:*

8 *'I know your deeds. Behold, I have put before you an open door which no one can shut, because you have a little power, and have kept My word, and have not denied My name.*

9 *'Behold, I will cause those of the synagogue of Satan, who say that they are Jews and are not, but lie—I will make them come and bow down at your feet, and make them know that I have loved you.*

10 *'Because you have kept the word of My perseverance, I also will keep you from the hour of testing, that hour which is about to come upon the whole world, to test those who dwell on the earth.*

11 *'I am coming quickly; hold fast what you have, so that no one will take your crown.*

12 *'He who overcomes, I will make him a pillar in the temple of My God, and he will not go out from it anymore; and I will write on him the name of My God, and the name of the city of My God, the new Jerusalem, which comes down out of heaven from My God, and My new name.*

13 *'He who has an ear, let him hear what the Spirit says to the churches.'*

Chapter 7
The Letter to Philadelphia

Philadelphia is the city everyone loves to love. Like Smyrna, Jesus has no word of rebuke for the church here, suggesting His approval of their responses to the culture in which they lived. Philadelphia was named after its founding brothers, Attalus and Eumenes, whose undying loyalty to each other earned them the moniker Philadelphus ("brotherly love").[1] Today, churches and Christians alike identify with the churches at Smyrna and Philadelphia. That's perfectly fine as long as we see ourselves in the other five churches as well. We must always keep in mind that the collection of all seven letters represent the Church at large, revealing her strengths and weaknesses. Keeping this in mind requires us to assess ourselves in the context of *each* letter. If we only see ourselves in the "good" churches, we're doing it wrong.

As we've seen in all the letters so far, Philadelphia's history played a vital role in Jesus's message to the church there. Archaeologist and New Testament scholar William Ramsay described Philadelphia as a "missionary city," standing as a doorway not only for trade but for introducing Greek language and culture to the east. He notes that

---

1   Grant, *Revelation*, 184.

the city was not built as a military stronghold, but instead was founded as a "centre of the Græco-Asiatic civilization...to promote a certain unity of spirit, customs, and loyalty within the realm." He adds that by 19 CE, "the Lydian tongue had ceased to be spoken in Lydia, and Greek was the only language of the country."[2] It seems Philadelphia was perfectly situated for the effective advancement of information and ideas, transforming an entire people group in a relatively short time.

Although it was a center of culture, Philadelphia remained one of the smaller and least wealthy cities in the region. Citizens called the surrounding countryside *Catacecaumene* ("burnt land"), because volcanic activity left "rivers of black lava and vast cinder-heaps."[3] However, the soil was rich with nutrients specifically suited for vineyards. Grapes and wine became the city's main export, tying Philadelphia's economic security to the consistent production of the "burnt land." While never growing to the prosperity of other cities, Philadelphia lived comfortably and in relative peace. Then, in 17 CE, an earthquake—one Pliny called "the greatest in human history"—devastated the region, leveling Philadelphia.[4] For years afterward, Philadelphia's population lived in terror of aftershocks. Strabo writes the city was "full of earthquakes," resulting in walls that "never cease to be cracked" and a city "constantly suffering damage." He adds that many refused to return to live in the city, choosing instead to "live as farmers in the countryside," content with life in "insecure dwellings" in and near the Catacecaumene.[5]

Rome responded to the natural disaster by sending aid. Caesar Tiberius suspended tax collection in the region for five years to help with economic recovery and rebuilding. As new emperors sat

---

2   Ramsay, *The Letters to the Seven Churches*, 391-392.
3   *ibid*, 396.
4   Pliny, as quoted in Hemer, *The Letters to the Seven Churches*, 156.
5   Strabo, as quoted in Hemer, *The Letters to the Seven Churches*, 156.

the throne, aid continued to flow into Philadelphia. That is, until Domitian came into power. Responding to yet another natural disaster (this time a wide-spread famine), Domitian ordered half of all vineyards to be cut down, and he forbade any new ones from being planted. Perhaps he thought the land could better serve the empire by producing wheat (something the Catacecaumene was ill-suited for). Perhaps he sought to enrich himself or ingratiate himself with Italian vine growers, helping them remain prosperous under harsh environmental conditions. Regardless of Domitian's motivation, his actions pulled the proverbial rug out from under Philadelphia, binding them in an economic straight jacket while a famine ravaged the realm. It was at this time that John's Revelation letter arrived, with Jesus introducing Himself to Philadelphia as "He who is holy, who is true."

Jesus: Ever Present, Ever Faithful

Jesus's introduction speaks directly to their current circumstances, and it overtly contrasts the institutions and groups exercising power over the church there. We've already discussed how Domitian's reinvigoration of the imperial cult threatened Christians who refused to participate. At best, believers would have their patriotism questioned. At worst, they would be declared enemies of the state. Domitian wanted to be worshiped as divine. Jesus declares He Himself alone is holy. Both Jesus and Domitian claimed divinity. However, Jesus is the only one who predicted His death and resurrection. Jesus died, was buried, and rose again on the third day. Jesus is who He says He is. Jesus is holy and divine. Domitian was not.

Jesus doubles down on His divinity, declaring He is also true. There are a number of definitions contained in the Greek word *alethinos* (al-ay-thee-**nos**), which is translated "true" here. First, it means "that which has not only the name and resemblance, but the real nature corresponding to the name." Domitian may *say* he and his family are divine, but Jesus actually *is* divine. He is *alethinos*, true. The second meaning would have been scandalous to first century hearers: "opposite to what is fictitious, counterfeit, imaginary, simulated or pretended."[6] By calling Himself true (*alethinos*), Jesus called Domitian a fake. Regardless of the power Domitian held, he was simply a pretender. Jesus is the name above every other name.

Let's imagine a couple of things here regarding Jesus's introduction as holy and true (especially considering the not-so-hidden meanings of "true"). It took an incredible amount of courage for John to both write those words and deliver them to seven cities. Seven strategic cities, mind you, placed at vital hubs of trade, ensuring the message contained in Revelation would travel far and wide. It also took an insane amount of courage for the church leader in Philadelphia to actually *read* this letter to the congregation. Calling Jesus, not Domitian, both holy and true would have been tantamount to sedition. Reading this letter would not have been viewed as merely an act of resistance, but of rebellion. There would be no exile or banishment for that charge. Only death.

At the same time, though, what a relief for the church in Philadelphia. Jesus, not Domitian, has divine authority. Jesus, not Domitian, has their best interests at heart. And while they may be struggling to make ends meet, they do meet more days than they don't. The storm rages, but Jesus is right there with them. He did not leave them. He did not forsake them. Jesus, not Domitian, is holy and true.

Jesus's claim of divinity not only resisted Domitian's declaration, but it also complicated the argument made by the Jewish population

---

6   James Strong, *Enhanced Strong's Lexicon* (Woodside Bible Fellowship, 1995).

that Jesus was a false Messiah. Christ's assertion to having "the key of David" goes even further, opposing their own claim of religious authority. The key of David gestures back to when the Lord deposed Shebna, the steward of the royal household, for Eliakim. Apparently, Shebna played fast and loose with the king's wealth, improving his own lifestyle rather than managing it for the king's benefit. Upon Eliakim, then, the Lord "set the key of the house of David...when he opens no one will shut, when he shuts no one will open."[7] Keys represent authority, and the Lord took authority from Shebna, and placed it solely upon Eliakim, foreshadowing the coming of Jesus who would be given all authority in heaven and earth.[8]

It's quite likely that leaders in the Jewish community shut Christians out of the synagogue. Jesus comforts His people, reminding them that He holds the keys to the Kingdom of God. He determines who gains entry, and He acts with absolute authority and sovereignty, independent of the will of man and irresistible by the power of man. The synagogue leaders could keep Christians from entering a building. Jesus has final say on who enters heaven. In that context, who has the greater authority?

Take Advantage of the Open Door

The church in Philadelphia may not have thought much of themselves. Jesus Himself said they had but "a little power," but a little power is all you need when the power of God is behind you. Like Smyrna, they endured suffering for their faith. Unlike Smyrna, Philadelphian believers also had to contend with a strained economy dependent on the goodwill of the state. When natural disasters rocked Philadelphia (first an earthquake, then a famine), many in the city blamed Christians for upsetting the gods. The

---

7   Isaiah 22:22.
8   See Matthew 28:18.

ensuing economic instability brought on by Domitian's vineyard policy only added fuel to that fire. That amount of pressure would make disappearing into the background of society an easy choice. To be sure, it's exactly what Sardis did. Out of sight, out of mind. Choosing to stay and minister is the more difficult choice. After all, new policies could come down from Rome at any time, further disabling people's ability to support themselves and their families. Not only that, but another "super quake" could destroy the city again, displacing the population. Just how much effort should be put into establishing roots under these circumstances? With all the unknowns swirling about, furthering the Kingdom of God may have been furthest from their mind.

When Jesus tells Philadelphia that He's set before them an open door that no one can shut, He isn't talking about access. He is talking about ministry. The New Testament often compares ministry work with open doors. Luke records Paul recounting his missionary work to the church at Antioch, describing it as God opening a "door of faith to the Gentiles."[9] In his first letter to the Corinthians, Paul explains his decision to stay at Ephesus, writing, "a wide door for effective service has opened to me."[10] To the Colossians, Paul asks for them to pray that "God will open up to us a door for the word."[11] Doors are synonymous with ministry, specifically with carrying out the Great Commission of preaching the gospel, baptizing believers, and making disciples.

Philadelphia had a perpetually open door—a door no one could shut—to promote the Kingdom of God and fulfill the commission of Christ for His Church. Indeed, the Great Commission seems to have aligned perfectly with the original premise of Philadelphia's founding. The propagation of ideas, languages, and culture was a

---

9   Acts 14:27.
10   1 Corinthians 16:8-9.
11   Colossians 4:3.

core component of the city's identity. The church in Philadelphia, then, was perfectly placed to promote the gospel of Jesus, not only in Philadelphia, but eastward toward Phrygia and all of Asia Minor. It certainly was a door that no man could shut!

Although no one could shut the door Jesus opened, obstacles could dissuade them from even attempting to walk through it. If there's one common denominator with ministry opportunities, it's adversity. Paul wrote that although a "wide door" of ministry lay open for him, there were "many adversaries" squaring off against him. However, Paul chose to stay in Ephesus, taking advantage of the open door regardless (or in spite of) the adversaries. Fear only sees adversity, obstacles, adversaries. Faith acknowledges those things, but chooses instead to focus on the opportunities and possibilities. Faith hopes for effective ministry, trusts God for results, and serves to the best of our ability so that the gospel reaches the world. Fear emphasizes why we can't. Faith remembers the words of the Lord through Isaiah: "No weapon that is formed against you will prosper; and every tongue that accuses you in judgment you will condemn. *This is the heritage of the servants of the Lord,* and their vindication is from Me."[12] Victory was the heritage of God's people then. Victory through faith in Jesus is the heritage of God's people now.

Christ's power is the catalyst for a successful ministry and a life of faith. The Philadelphia church was small, possessing no great wealth or influence, but they stayed close to Jesus. They kept His Word and never denied His name. They did not have much, but what they did have was more than enough. Commenting on Philadelphia's situation, Wiersbe wrote, "It's not the size or strength of a church that determines its ministry, but faith in the call and command of the Lord."[13] Philadelphia was faithful to Christ, but

---

12   Isaiah 54:17, emphasis added.
13   Wiersbe, *The Bible Exposition Commentary,* 578.

they hesitated to take full advantage of the open door He set before them. They had allowed fear to place limits on their ministry. Jesus encouraged them to take the chance and trust Him.

If God opens a door, nothing and no one can stop us from going through it. But we must *choose* to go through it. It's a scary endeavor, because walking through doors means leaving the known for a hallway of the unknown. It's challenging, and we often feel unprepared, unequipped, and unworthy of the work. It can feel impossible at times. But all things are possible to those who believe.[14]

Jesus responds to Philadelphia's hesitancy with a subtle, indeed gentle, rebuke. Of all the cities, Philadelphia was the best placed for promoting the gospel eastward through Asia Minor, opening even more doors in Byzantium (modern-day Istanbul) and the port cities along the coast of the Black Sea. That's easy to say now, almost two thousand years later, in a comfy seat with a book in our hand. But to the Philadelphian believers, the door opened into a vast unknown. Success in ministry is not guaranteed, but to quote the great Wayne Gretzky (the current record holder for goals in a career and season in the National Hockey League), "You miss every shot you don't take." If we wait to have every contingency planned for and every question answered, we will never walk through the doors God opens for us. God only gave Abraham a direction when He called him out of his homeland, not a destination. How many of us would energetically and eagerly answer *that* call? I shudder to think of how many opportunities are missed because we are afraid of the unknown beyond the open door.

Part of Jesus's counsel to Philadelphia echoes what He told Thyatira: "hold fast what you have." What did they have? His name, His Word, a little power, and an open door. That's all they needed.

---

14   Mark 9:23.

That's all we need. Let's step through the doors of ministry open to us. Both collectively as a Church and individually as believers, let's commit to stepping forward into the unknown with faith and courage, singing the refrain of the old hymnal:

> Little is much when God is in it,
> Labor not for wealth or fame;
> There's a crown, and you can win it,
> If you go in Jesus's name.[15]

Power, like control, is an illusion. When Pilate asserted that he had the power to crucify or release Jesus, Christ responded, "You could have no authority over Me, unless it had been given you from above."[16] No person—indeed, no group, government, or state—wields power of their own making. Only Christ Himself possesses all power and authority; and He delegates to whom He wills. Never forget who opened the door. If God is for us, who can stand against us!

A Promise of Protection and Permanence

Philadelphians (not just the church there) were a people always on the lookout for the next bad thing: natural disaster, Roman proclamation, economic failure, etc. Life in Philadelphia was peaceful and unsettling at the same time. Christ sets His people's minds at ease, indicating their future is sealed and held in His own hand. Believers in the empire were in the minority, oppressed by the state, marginalized by society, and ostracized by many in the Jewish population. Christians did not amount to much in the socio-political and religious landscapes, but Christ's consolation indicates not everything is as it seems. Those in power now will soon be powerless, those who oppress now will soon be judged,

---

15   Kittie L. Suffield. "Little is Much When God is in It." 1924. Hymnary. Accessed November 9, 2022. https://hymnary.org/text/in_the_harvest_field_now_ripened.
16   John 19:10-11.

those who slander and exclude will soon be found wanting. There may be a thumb on the scales of justice now, but do not fear; Jesus is King of Kings and Lord of Lords. His is the last word.

Just like in His letter to Smyrna, Jesus takes the position that the Jews oppressing His church are, in fact, a synagogue of Satan. John the Baptist once called Jews in his audience a "brood of vipers," warning their status as sons of Abraham won't keep them from God's judgment because "from these stones God is able to raise up children of Abraham."[17] Jesus references a blessing recorded in Isaiah meant to comfort Israel:

> The sons of those who afflicted you will come bowing to you, and all those who despised you will bow themselves at the soles of your feet; and they will call you the city of the Lord, the Zion of the Holy One of Israel.[18]

Christ takes this blessing and imparts it on His Church, asserting that the physical Israel will one day bow before the spiritual. "Humble yourself in the sight of the Lord," James wrote, "and He will lift you up."[19]

Jesus created a Kingdom on earth comprised of Jews and Gentiles, men and women, enslaved and free people of every tribe, nation, and language interacting as equals, as peers, as family. The world holds on to its hierarchies and castes now, but one day Christ will erase them all. Jesus is not suggesting that Christians will be worshiped by anyone. Only God is worthy of worship. The word picture He creates signifies that accusers and oppressors will one day acknowledge their folly. In that day, every worldly power dynamic will dissolve, and "the meek will inherit the earth."[20]

---

17   Matthew 3:7-9.
18   Isaiah 60:14.
19   James 4:10.
20   Matthew 5:5.

Christians endure hardship in the world because there is enmity between the world and God. The Kingdom of God will always be a separated people. The Holy Spirit resides in believers, marking them as separated for service and holy to the Lord. Kingdom people are different by design, and that difference is a constant cause of friction between believers and the world. However, the world will face its own judgment, and Jesus promised the Philadelphian church protection from "the hour of testing…which is about to come upon the whole world."[21] There are two ways to interpret this promise. Either the world will suffer while the Church watches on, unaffected by global calamities, or the Church will not be here at all while the world is "tested." Both interpretations assert Christ's protection of His Church from global suffering during the period described in the large middle portion of Revelation (commonly known as "The Tribulation"). His promise encourages believers to look beyond current circumstances, believing in an eternal future already established in heaven.

Jesus promises security for all whose faith remains steadfast. He utilizes language and imagery particular to Philadelphian believers who live in constant fear of aftershocks. Many Philadelphians lived outside of the city, because an earthquake could bring their home down around them at any moment. In heaven, Christians won't have to worry about instability of any kind. They will be able to remain within the city, eternally secure in their Lord. Heaven will never fall; it will be their eternal home, and they shall be pillars in it. In architectural language, pillars and arches were the highest technology available upon which to build. Indeed, many ancient ruins today are just the pillars of buildings that fell long ago. What a beautiful way to describe our eternal existence: immovable, permanent, firmly-planted pillars in the city of our God.

---

21   Revelation 3:10.

For Philadelphians, not even the *name* of their city was secure. In the first century alone, the city changed its name at least three times in deference to the emperor who provided aid. Jesus also implies permanence when promising to write three names on all believers in heaven: "the name of my God, and the name of the city of My God…and My new name."[22] In heaven, the new Jerusalem shall bear the name of God who is unchanging. Philadelphian believers lived in a world that was unsettled and insecure. Nothing could be trusted to last. No one could be trusted to remain faithful to their word. All they had (or so they thought) was the moment in which they lived, so they treasured and protected it. On the other side of eternity, however, all of that changes. For those who overcome, what once was an unsettled life becomes permanent for all eternity.

Philadelphia may have felt as if they had a little power, but they had been endued with power from on high. Sometimes, in order to embrace that power and walk in it, Christians have to lift their eyes toward heaven and their assured hope. Keeping Christ in view—walking close to Him—may not diminish the powers at work around us, but it will remind us of the power at work in us. With Him, all things are possible.

Philadelphia was on shaky ground, literally and figuratively. The idea of permanence and rootedness must have been foreign concepts to a people who didn't know if their home would last the day or if some power (natural or political) would pull the proverbial rug from under them again. Their environment was chaotic and ever-changing, but their faith remained steadfast. What a witness against any of us who might consider our own circumstances as justification to compromise our faith or resist Christ's call to reach the world with the gospel.

---

22   Revelation 3:12.

The worries of Philadelphia feel all too familiar. At the time of this writing (late 2022), the world is still overcoming a global pandemic that has killed over 6.6 million people and counting since its outbreak in 2020.[23] Natural disasters like earthquakes, hurricanes, tsunamis, and wildfires have wreaked havoc in cities throughout the world. Horrific acts of violence have snuffed out far too many lives all too soon. Earlier this year, Vladimir Putin sent an army into Ukraine, attempting to force them back into the fold of the old Russian empire. When that didn't work, he sent bombs and bomb-laden drones to terrorize the Ukrainian people. The world seems saturated with death, wars, and rumors of wars, leaving brokenness and trauma in their wake.

These times are not unprecedented, but they are uncertain. And it's in these uncertain times (or perhaps *for* them), Jesus has placed an open door before His Church. God grants each of us exactly what is required to fulfill His will in—and for—our lives. Little is much when God is in it. The world worries what the future holds. We can introduce them to the One who holds the future. Whenever we feel as if our efforts are in vain, as if we are entirely too small to affect any amount of change in the world, remember: His Kingdom is established; His city cannot be shaken; His people shall not be moved. There is a crown, and you can win it, if you go in Jesus's name.

Let this chapter be your catalyst.
Go.
In Jesus's name.

---

23   Worldometer. Accessed November 9, 2022. https://www.worldometers.info/coronavirus.

Revelation 3:14–22

14 *"To the angel of the church in Laodicea write: The Amen, the faithful and true Witness, the Beginning of the creation of God, says this:*

15 *'I know your deeds, that you are neither cold nor hot; I wish that you were cold or hot.*

16 *'So because you are lukewarm, and neither hot nor cold, I will spit you out of My mouth.*

17 *'Because you say, "I am rich, and have become wealthy, and have need of nothing," and you do not know that you are wretched and miserable and poor and blind and naked,*

18 *I advise you to buy from Me gold refined by fire so that you may become rich, and white garments so that you may clothe yourself, and that the shame of your nakedness will not be revealed; and eye salve to anoint your eyes so that you may see.*

19 *'Those whom I love, I reprove and discipline; therefore be zealous and repent.*

20 *'Behold, I stand at the door and knock; if anyone hears My voice and opens the door, I will come in to him and will dine with him, and he with Me.*

21 *'He who overcomes, I will grant to him to sit down with Me on My throne, as I also overcame and sat down with My Father on His throne.*

22 *'He who has an ear, let him hear what the Spirit says to the churches.' "*

Chapter 8

The Letter to Laodicea

The church at Laodicea has the distinction of being the only one with no redeeming qualities noted in its letter. Even Sardis—who had a name that they were alive but were actually spiritually dead—had a small remnant of faithful people, "things that remain" that could be strengthened. Laodicea receives not even that subtle commendation. They had fully immersed themselves into the sea of relevance and were in danger of drowning. Worse still, they were completely blind to their true state, believing themselves to be blessed by God when in fact they barely associated themselves with Him at all. The church embraced the philosophy and ideals of the city, celebrating independence and elevating the trappings of wealth as the goal to be pursued.

Laodicea: A City Like No Other

First-century Laodicea was an extravagantly wealthy city. It was the most significant of the tri-city cluster that included Colossae and Hierapolis.[1] More than any of the seven cities in Revelation, Laodicea profited from its location along trade routes. Similar to Philadelphia, Laodicea was meant to be a missionary city promoting Greek culture and language eastward into Phrygia. Instead, Laodicea became a center for banking and finances. Ramsay notes that Phrygia was the least Hellenized of all of Asia Minor, still speaking its native language and "little affected by Greek manners."[2] Under Roman rule (beginning in 133 BCE), and especially during Cicero's time as proconsul (51-50 BCE), Laodicea's wealth and influence grew. Scholars like Ramsay and Hemer point to Cicero's cashing in bills of exchange as indicative of the city's vast wealth. The culture of Laodicea was one of pliability, a willingness to bend a little or a lot for the sake of trade and profit—not exactly conducive for spreading Greek culture into foreign lands, but perfectly suited for international business relations.

Other than banking, two exports (black wool and medical salves) pushed the city into the foreground of Asia Minor and much of the Roman empire. The wool was not just dark in color. Strabo records that Laodicean sheep produced wool with remarkable softness, shine, and "raven-black colour" of high demand, creating a consistent flow of "splendid revenue" for those in the garment industry.[3] The city was also well known for a medical school, and Laodicean coins were stamped with names of leading physicians. Laodicea also produced components used in eye and ear ointments, which were widely sold.[4] Those three pillars of economic strength (banking, wool, and medicine) shored up Laodicea against any financial strains the region may face.

---

1   Paul refers to this group of cities in Colossians 4:13. They were so close that he instructs his letter to the Colossians to be read and Laodicea and for the Colossians to read his letter from Laodicea (perhaps Philemon).

2   Ramsay, *Letters to the Seven Churches*, 415.

3   Strabo as qtd. in Hemer, *Letters*, 199.

4   Ramsay, 417.

Not even nature could bring the city down, but an earthquake did almost destroy Laodicea in 60 CE. However, rather than accept aid from Rome (like Philadelphia did after the earthquake in 17 CE), Laodicea took the unprecedented measure of rebuilding on its own. Roman historian, Tacitus writes, "Laodicea, one of the famous Asiatic cities, was laid in ruins by an earthquake, but recovered by its own resources, without assistance from ourselves."[5] Even more striking, Laodicea intentionally declined aid offered by the Senate and the emperor. Could you imagine that happening today? A large city gets decimated by a natural disaster and then *refuses* help from the government? Inconceivable!

Generosity from Laodiceans, particularly those of great wealth, not only rebuilt the city but improved upon it. In fact, most of the ruins existing on the site of Laodicea today are of buildings constructed after the earthquake. For example, a large stadium bears the name Nicostratus, indicating he was the one who funded, designed, or built it.[6] The city-wide reconstruction project engaged the entire population in philanthropic endeavors, donating time, talent, labor, and finances. Hemer writes their generosity itself is not noteworthy, but the "scale and ostentation of the donations" make Laodicea unique.[7] The people relished their independence and seemed to embrace the opportunity to put it on display by refusing financial aid from Rome. The church in Laodicea adopted the same independent attitude, trusting in its own ability, and refusing spiritual aid from the Lord.

Then Jesus sent them a letter.

Jesus presents Himself to Laodicea using three specific but intertwined titles: "the Amen, the faithful and true Witness, and the

---

5   Tacitus, *Annals* (14.27.1).
6   Hemer, *Leters to the Seven Churches*, 194.
7   *ibid.*

beginning of the creation of God."[8] Amen is a transliterated word meaning "truth" or "true" in both the Hebrew and Greek. Through Isaiah, the Lord laments Israel's rebelliousness and promises both judgment for the wicked and protection for the faithful, declaring they will be "blessed by the God of truth (*amen*)."[9] In John's gospel, Jesus declares Himself as "the Way, the Truth, and the Life."[10] In this letter, He is—again—the Truth, bearing the authority, omniscience, and righteousness of God. Jesus expands on this notion by also calling Himself the "faithful and true Witness." Christ is trustworthy as a witness because He is a true witness, obtaining the highest possible sense of the term. Theologian Richard Chenevix Trench argues there are three things necessary to be called a true witness: "[first] to have seen with His own eyes what He attests; [second] to be competent to relate it for others; [third] to be willing truthfully to do so."[11] Jesus more than fulfils every condition.

Jesus is the perfect witness because He can never lie. He is also the preeminent witness because He is omnipresent, the "beginning of the creation of God."[12] Jesus is the origin and initiator of creation. We find a more complete understanding of that in Paul's letter to the Colossians:

> *[Jesus] is the image of the invisible God, the firstborn of all creation. For by Him all things were created, both in the heavens and in the earth, visible and invisible...all things have been created through Him and for Him. He is before all things, and in Him all things hold together.*[13]

Jesus is the Source of all things, the Alpha and Omega that initiated the beginning of everything. He sees all and knows all. Jesus is

---

8   Revelation 3:14.
9   Isaiah 65:16.
10   John 14:6.
11   Trench as qtd. in Jamieson et al, *Commentary Critical and Explanatory on the Whole Bible*, 561.
12   Revelation 3:14.
13   Colossians 1:15-17.

Truth. He is Faithful. He is the perfect Witness. And He has a word for Laodicea.

Dear Laodicea: You're Making Me Sick.

Jesus describes the Laodicean church as neither cold nor hot. And lest you think I'm being too harsh with the section title, Jesus told them He would spit (literally vomit) them out of His mouth, because they were lukewarm. Grant Osborne argues that because Laodicea faced "no external pressure from pagan or Jewish persecution (like Sardis, Smyrna, or Philadelphia)" and "no internal threat from heretical movements (like Ephesus, Pergamum, or Thyatira), they had succumbed to their own affluent lifestyle, and they did not even know it!"[14] They had deeds (Jesus saw them) but it wasn't just their activity Jesus was sick over. It was them. Their character, their faith, their love for God and for people, everything about the church in Laodicea was nauseatingly lukewarm.

I've heard teaching and read commentaries that explain "hot," "cold," and "lukewarm" as indicating spiritual fervency. Wiersbe calls them "three spiritual temperatures."[15] Allegory is a potent interpretive process (or hermeneutic), but here it forces meaning onto those terms. When we consider that Jesus desired Laodicea to be either hot or cold, we have to wonder, "Would Jesus want *anyone* to be spiritually cold?" Wiersbe addresses this potential flaw in the allegory, arguing "at least he would feel it!"[16] But would they? Did the Jews who cried out for Jesus's crucifixion feel spiritually cold? It could be argued they were acting with the utmost zeal, protecting against heresy and blasphemy. How about the Roman soldiers who nailed Jesus to the cross? Cold? Indifferent (lukewarm)? The

---

14   Osborne, *Revelation*, 207.
15   Wiersbe, *The Bible Exposition Commentary*, 580.
16   *ibid.*

comparison of Jesus's terms to spiritual temperatures falls apart when we being to apply them to different groups, because each group acts within their own set of contexts, their own lived experiences. People may feel spiritually "hot," but the spirit giving them heat may not be the Holy Spirit. So, if Jesus was not describing Laodicea's spiritual temperature, what was He doing?

By describing Laodicea as lukewarm, Jesus used language His audience would immediately understand and connect with. The city, as wealthy as it was, depended entirely on outside sources for their water. Underwater aqueducts ran from cities like Colossae and Hierapolis. (So much for independence, right?) Colossae was known for its pure, cold water, while Hierapolis was known for its hot springs. "So the hot waters of Hierapolis were medicinal," writes Hemer, "the cold waters of Colossae pure and life-giving."[17] However, by the time water from either city reached Laodicea, it had lost its original nature, having become lukewarm and useless for anything. In fact, the water was often foul and undrinkable, potentially dangerous. The church in Laodicea matched its water supply. What was meant to be life-giving had become foul and potentially dangerous. By disconnecting from their Source, the church lost what made them valuable to the people and useful in the Kingdom of God.

Wiersbe applies thermodynamics to make an astute observation about the notion of lukewarmness. He cites the second law of thermodynamics, writing, "unless something [energy] is added from the outside [of a system], the system decays and dies."[18] For example, water heaters depend on fire to make water hot. A refrigerator depends on electricity to keep itself cold. Should the fire or electricity be removed from either "system," the water

17   Hemer, *Letters to the Seven Churches*, 187.
18   Wiersbe, *Bible Exposition Commentary*, 580

will cool and the refrigerator will heat up, eventually becoming the temperature of their surroundings. The church in Laodicea disconnected from its source of spiritual energy. Without the Holy Spirit, they became lukewarm, a spiritual liability in the city, and they didn't even know it. Even worse, they believed they were spiritually fervent, seeing everything around them as confirmation of their blessed state. Jesus said, "Without Me, you can do nothing."[19] The church said, "I'm rich and have need of nothing." Shockingly, the Laodicean church had been without Christ for years and was oblivious.

Honestly, that shouldn't be too much of a surprise. It wasn't unprecedented. The Old Testament tells of when Israel endured a time of exile in Babylon because of their consistent rebellion against the Lord. Ezekiel was a prophet during that time, forced to live in Babylon. While there, he received a number of visions from the Lord showing the remnant in Israel continuing to sin and participating in pagan worship. They had even raised idols and statues inside the temple of the Lord! One day, God led Ezekiel in a vision to the temple. Ezekiel records what he saw there, writing what might be the most heartbreaking words in the Old Testament: "Then the glory of the Lord departed from the threshold of the temple."[20] God had left the temple, and nobody noticed. In fact, when the Lord left the temple, the *only* person who knew was Ezekiel, and he was in Babylon.

Wealth replaced the Holy Spirit as the power behind the Laodicean church. Let's face it, money is powerful. It grants access and status. It opens doors and greases wheels. If you have it, certain worries disappear into the realm of assumptions. Thing like food, water, clothing, and a home are taken for granted. Money ensures

---

19   John 15:5.
20   Ezekiel 10:15.

that businesses run, that restaurant lights stay on, and the church doors remain open. Money is power, or so it seems. But it's all a lie, especially to the Church.

Abundance tricked the Laodicean church into thinking it was self-sufficient, in need of nothing. A church that sees no need is a church that is dying quickly. Sardis saw God's blessing in their religious activity. They thought they were alive, but they were spiritually dead. Laodicea saw God's blessing in their financial prosperity. That made them not only dead but dangerous. Please catch this: the Laodicean church was not a danger to themselves. Lukewarm water does not harm itself. The Laodicean church was a danger to others, to the very people Jesus commissioned His Church to reach with the gospel. Rather than bringing life-giving water to people of Laodicea, the church was bringing tepid, dangerous water. No wonder Jesus was about to vomit them out!

The church thought they were rich, but they were in fact wretchedly poor, blind, and naked.[21] They ignored Jesus's teaching on prosperity. He calls money "unrighteous wealth," declaring "you cannot serve God and wealth."[22] Laodicea sought affluence, found it, and called themselves blessed. Jesus says, "Blessed are those who hunger and thirst after righteousness."[23] Laodicea adopted the business model of the world, which measures success by profit margins. They saw prosperity as a fruit of the Spirit. To be sure, there may have been activity in the church, but there was no power, no "unction from the Holy One."[24] Without it, without power and anointing, without that outside source of energy coming from God Himself, spiritual fervency dies, and we begin taking on the

---

21   Notice that Jesus addresses Laodicea's three sources of revenue: banking, eye ointment, and the garment industry.
22   Luke 16:11 & 13.
23   Matthew 5:6.
24   1 John 2:20.

spiritual "temperature" of our surroundings. That's not relevance. That's death. The church in Laodicea had become septic and didn't know it.

Pursue True Riches

The church did not fall accidentally or incidentally into their state of independence. In his letter to the Colossians, Paul admonishes the bishop of Laodicea, Archippus, writing, "Take heed to the ministry which you have received in the Lord, that you may fulfill it."[25] Apparently, word got to Paul that ministry had been lacking in the city of prosperity. Self-sufficiency was the Laodicean church's starting point. Believers in the city grew up with a flourishing economy that provided numerous opportunities for promotion. They lived as a people who prided themselves on independence, celebrating their own innovation and progress after the earthquake in 60 CE. Christ's letter advises them to shed that core aspect of their identity, adopting reliance on Him as the proper replacement. His counsel gestures toward a spiritual economy upon which believers depend, whether they know it or not.

Convinced of its own wealth, Laodicea was blind to its own poverty.[26] Jesus doesn't mind His followers being wealthy, but wealth had produced a certain "smug self-satisfaction" in believers at Laodicea.[27] Accumulating wealth had actually rendered believers spiritually wretched and poor. Jesus counsels them to purchase from Him gold refined by fire. They needed to pursue a different form of currency, a different type of wealth, namely faith. Peter writes that faith is "more precious than gold…even though tested by fire."[28] He, like other New Testament authors, exhorts his readers

25   Colossians 4:17.
26   Barclay, *The Revelation of John*, 143.
27   Osborne, *Revelation*, 206-207.
28   1 Peter 1:7.

to rejoice in suffering, implying that trials act as a purifying agent for faith in the same way fire is for gold and other precious metals. Faith, then, is the gold which Jesus wants Laodicea to pursue. Pure faith, tried by fire—purified by suffering—needs to be our main pursuit. In the context of eternity, it is the only gold that endures and the only precious metal that makes one rich.

Jesus's counsel to buy white garments challenged the city's garment economy, which benefited from the unique black wool of Laodicean sheep. In our chapter on Sardis, we learned that white garments signified victory, specifically Christ's victory over sin and death, a victory in which we share. White garments also signify the righteousness of Christ covering our own unrighteousness. Isaiah rejoices that God "has clothed me with garments of salvation," including a "robe of righteousness."[29] Paul exhorts the Ephesians and Colossians to "put on the new man," suggesting a shedding of the old self and a wearing of the new.[30] The clothing metaphor runs throughout Scripture, beginning in Genesis when God replaces the hand-made fig leaf coverings with garments of skins. Indeed, God's purpose for making those skins matches exactly with Christ's offer of white garments: "so that the shame of your nakedness will not be revealed."[31] This goes beyond the connection between nakedness and humiliation. In the ancient world, defeated foes were often forced to march naked, intensifying their defeat. Christ's garments don't cover our bodies, they cover our grime-covered souls. His robe of righteousness covers our unrighteousness, making it possible for us to be in the presence of a holy God. Trying to hide our unrighteousness with rich clothing is like the proverbial "ring of gold in a swine's snout."[32] It doesn't work. The finest wool in the

---

29   Isaiah 61:10.
30   Ephesians 4:24 and Colossians 3:10.
31   Revelation 3:18.
32   Proverbs 11:22.

world can't cover sin. Only the white garments purchased from Jesus cover our soul's nakedness.

Lastly, Jesus wanted Laodicean believers to buy eye salve from Him, "so that you may see."[33] Despite the city's connection to a valuable and effectual eye ointment, the church there remained spiritually blind. Affluence has both a numbing and blinding effect. The Laodicean church could neither see their own plight nor discern the spiritual state of others.[34] The only remedy for spiritual blindness is the ointment Christ offers. Jesus began His ministry proclaiming "recovery of sight to the blind."[35] He meant it in both the literal and figurative sense, as He healed many who were both literally and spiritually blind. Ironically, healing those who were physically blind often exposed the spiritual blindness of religious people who claimed spiritual sight.[36] Being blind while claiming sight is both foolish and dangerous. Jesus warned, "if a blind man guides a blind man, both will fall into a pit."[37] A spiritually blind church is a danger to itself and others. Laodicea needed healing; and only Christ is the source of all spiritually healing.

To begin healing, Laodicea needed to shift its reliance off the sources of affluence prevalent in the city. Jesus advises them to buy His gold, His white garments, His eye salve. So, what exactly do these things cost? Well, nothing…and everything. It costs nothing because salvation can't be bought. The cross is a gift from God to you, to me, to all of us—a gift given by grace and accepted through faith. There is nothing we possess valuable enough to be a fair exchange for what God offers us through Jesus. So, faith costs us nothing; but following Jesus costs us everything. Jesus taught that

---

33   Revelation 3:18.
34   Beale, *The Book of Revelation*, 305.
35   Luke 4:18.
36   See Osborn, *Revelation*, 210.
37   Matthew 15:14.

anyone who follows Him must deny themselves. He modeled a life that put Himself last—with God first and others second—and said, "Follow Me." He left family and home fulfilling God's will in His life, ultimately leading to His death, and He said, "Follow Me." Faith in Jesus costs us nothing. Following Jesus costs us everything. One does not exist without the other. Maybe this is why Jesus says, "It's easier for a camel to go through the eye of a needle than for a rich man to enter the kingdom of God."[38] It's not impossible, but it's extraordinarily difficult.

Jesus levels His harshest rebuke against the Laodicean church: you're not wealthy, you're wretched and poor; you're not healthy, you're sick and a danger to yourself and others. What an utter shock this must have been as it was being read to the gathered church. How entirely confounded must they have been? How close to giving up altogether?

Then He told them He loved them.

Jesus says, "Those whom I love, I reprove and discipline."[39] The Laodicean church was indeed lost, but not hopelessly lost. They weren't outside of Christ's love. They had abandoned Jesus's provision, proudly declaring they "have need of nothing." They had folded independence and self-sufficiency into the culture of the Kingdom of God. They had essentially pushed Christ out of the church, and Jesus still loved them. Jesus loves the defeated church as much as the victorious church. He loved Laodicea and Sardis just as much as He loved Philadelphia and Smyrna. This is the beauty of Christ's love and the power of His grace. Nobody—no church, no believer, no person—is too far gone for Christ's love and grace to reach them.

---

38   Matthew 19:24, Mark 10:25, and Luke 18:25.
39   Revelation 3:19.

Promise of Fellowship

Jesus pivots so sharply from condemnation to love that Ramsay concludes these final verses (starting at verse nineteen) are, in fact, "an epilogue to the Seven Letters" rather than part of the Laodicean letter itself.[40] However, the letter to Laodicea (in its entirety) fits the model set in the previous six letters, so we are left to conclude these final lines are meant for the Laodicean believers. After severely rebuking them, Jesus reinforces His love for them like a parent to their child. I find that the best parents will shower their kids with love after having scolded or punished them for some offense. Because they love their children, parents will reprove and discipline them. Then, to *show* their love, those same parents will often scoop their children up in a warm hug. These last verses of the Laodicean letter are Jesus's hug for the church. Jesus finished reproving and disciplining; now He stands and knocks.

Jesus knocking on Laodicea's door carried significant meaning to the original hearers of the letter. Hemer notes that Laodicea, as a capital of the region, housed many troops in the city, and that early Roman law imposed the quartering of both troops and staff upon the citizens. Families were expected to provide food and housing, a daily monetary stipend or per diem, and—as if this were not enough—to provide "clothing and subsidies" to the officers.[41] By the end of the first century, the practice and exploitation of forced quartering had all but ended, but the laws remained, looming over households and fomenting distrust, animosity, and fear. A stranger knocking on the door evoked a sense of doom in Laodicea. Refusing to open the door was not an option. Opening it meant the family could go without to appease their intruders.

---

40   Ramsay, *Letters to the Seven Churches*, 430.
41   Hemer, *Letters to the Seven Churches*, 202.

In contrast, Jesus—the Son of God—knocks on the door, waiting to be let in. He does not impose Himself, but He does call out. And to those who hear His voice and open the door, Jesus promises an intimate time of fellowship. The Greek word used for "sup" is *deipneo* (dipe-**neh**-o) which is derived from *deipnon,* the chief meal held in the evening. Barclay notes that people "lingered" over this meal since it came at the end of the day's labor.[42] In the ancient world, sharing this meal was to "share a life."[43] It was a meal enjoyed with family and friends, very different from the meals taken by quartered troops. "You are my friends," Jesus says, "if you do what I command you."[44] And what did Jesus command His followers to do? "Love one another just as I have loved you."[45] His yoke is easy. His burden, light. His heart longs for restored fellowship, but He will not force it. Laodicean Christians, believing they had all they needed, pushed Jesus outside the church, resulting in a people who were lackluster, lukewarm, and dangerous. But Jesus was not done with them. He still loved them and desired *deipneo* with His people. He stands on the outside of the church, knocking and waiting for someone—anyone—to open the door.

It is possible to interpret *deipneo* as pointing toward the marriage supper of the Lamb recorded later in Revelation. The imagery surrounding the marriage supper is indeed similar: the Church—as a bride—is clothed in "fine linen, bright and clean," much like the white robes Jesus exhorts the Laodiceans to buy from Him.[46] Teachings and parables of Jesus that find their fulfillment in the marriage supper of the Lamb also connect with the Laodicean

---

42   Barclay, *The Revelation of John*, 147-148.
43   Osborn, *Revelation*, 213.
44   John 15:14.
45   John 15:12.
46   Revelation 19:8-9.

supper promised by Christ.[47] However, the image of Jesus standing and knocking suggests a more immediate application. Both verbs are written in the present tense. Jesus is standing at the door, knocking *right now*. The fellowship Jesus calls all of us into is not only a future hope but a present reality. We can enjoy His company today and every day. Osborne writes, "The promise here is of acceptance, sharing, and blessing, a deep fellowship with the One offering forgiveness and reconciliation."[48] Laodicea had shut Jesus out and tuned Him out. They no longer stood with Him, nor did they care to follow Him. Yet, there He is, knocking and calling out, waiting for anyone to open the door, so the relationship they once enjoyed together could be restored.

The Laodicean church succumbed to the trappings of wealth and power. They threw their lot in with the powers of state, of economy, and of the world. They forgot that Jesus said, "All authority is given to Me" and promised that the Church is "endued with power from on high."[49] The Laodicean church traded eternal authority with temporal authority. They may have gained the world, but they were in danger of losing their soul. Grasping at power in this world is futile since, ultimately, Christ is the only One with power. His promises suggest our energies are best spent living within the power already granted us, and with our eyes firmly fixed on our eternal reward. When we remember that Jesus offers for us to sit with Him on His throne, everything the world offers pales in comparison.

What was true for Laodicea is also true for you. You are not too lost for Jesus to find, too entrenched in the world for Him to love. Regardless of our reasons for abandoning Him, He is still

---

47   See The Parable of the Marriage Feast in Matthew 22 and The Parable of the Dinner in
      Luke 14. In both stories, the original invitees are unwilling to attend. In response, the ruler
      has invitations sent to the general population, the proverbial "unwashed masses" from all
      walks of life and social stations.
48   Osborn, *Revelation*, 213.
49   Matthew 28:18 and Luke 24:49 respectively.

the Good Shepherd, leaving the ninety-nine to find the lost one.[50] Jesus stands at the proverbial door, knocking and calling out for all who have shut Him out of their lives. None of us need to fear opening the door to Him. Unlike the Roman soldiers in Laodicea, Jesus wants to share with us, not take from us. He wants to connect deeply with each of His followers, and it's that connection which empowers us to face our daily lives with enduring faith.

All we have to do is open the door and let Him in.

---

50 Matthew 18:12-14

Conclusion

*Jesus actually expects those He's rescued to
live like His followers.*
                        - Pastor Rich Villodas

As a book, Revelation is apocalyptic, meaning it details the end of
the world and the coming judgment. The Revelation letters express
that judgment starts with the Church, and it starts now. Jesus, whose
eyes are a flame of fire[1]; whose judgments are true and righteous[2];
who sees not as man but as the almighty and all-knowing God[3];
Jesus clearly sees His Church, and we all would be wise to listen to
His judgment.

The Church represents Christ as His living, breathing, active body
on earth. We are supposed to influence our culture, expressing the
love of God for the world. We're not meant to be in the background,
silently watching and condemning the world. "Go into all the world,"
Jesus commanded, "and preach the gospel." Yet, since the days of
Constantine, the Church has consistently interpreted that as pointing
out and poking the specks in people's eyes, while ignoring the logs in

---

1   Revelation 1:14.
2   Psalms 19:9.
3   1 Samuel 16:7.

our own. That equates to over fifteen hundred years of harm caused by the Church. If we want to do better (and we should), we *must* allow Jesus to examine us like He did these churches, revealing our flaws and shortcomings so they can be corrected.

The Revelation letters show that every church thought their response to the dominant culture was correct. Each thought they were doing exactly what Jesus wanted them—and every other church—to be doing. However, out of the seven approaches detailed in these letters, only two were close to Jesus's ideal. And both of them came with a great cost: poverty, martyrdom, and a lifetime of being social pariahs. However, these were the marks of *successful* ministry in Jesus' eyes.

Each of the other five churches needed correction—some more stern than others. All five were in danger of spiritual death because of how they chose to respond to their culture. Seeking to save their lives, they were near to losing their faith.

These letters show that Christians will always find themselves at odds with the socio-political structures at work, because how the world does things greatly differs from how the Lord does them (or wants them done). They also show that Jesus has a message for His Church. But is the Church listening? Are we?

Evergreen faith is not a passive condition—it's an intentional choice. It's remembering that Jesus not only sees what we are doing, He see why. He sees the cultural environment and what His people endure. For faith to be evergreen, we must remember that Jesus promises eternal joy, peace, and life in His presence. Those promises are our hope, and that hope is an anchor for our souls, come what may. Hardships, while painful, serve to strengthen and grow our faith. For faith to last through struggles and the ever-changing tide of culture, we must fix our eyes on Jesus, His Word, and His promises. We won't always get it right, but we can never stop trying.

For as long as the Church is on the earth, Jesus actively works in and among her. He is intimately acquainted with His people. Jesus refers to each city's history in His letters to them. Their struggles were not unseen, their cries were not unheard. He clearly saw them and knew everything they had been through. Ramsay wrote that the original hearers of these letters "could not fail to discover in them the reference to his own city's history."[4] They could identify themselves in the letters and see how Christ's message, counsel, and promise immediately applied to their lives.

Remarkably, I have found that we also can see ourselves in these letters. We, too, have compromised, conformed, or overcompensated. We see the sparkle of wealth, and hear its siren's song. We endure hardship and feel anxiety. In short, we're human. In the same way, Jesus wants us to know that He deeply understands *our* histories, our joys as well as our traumas. Jesus has been with us through them all, and He is not done with us.

He is not done with you.

You are not too far gone for His grace to reach you. Nor are you so sanctified there is nothing for the Holy Spirit to correct. Jesus is watching and responding to His Church and His people. Jesus is still walking among the lampstands, among His people, convicting, consoling, correcting, knocking on doors—engaged, active, and present.

Those who have an ear to hear, let them hear what the Spirit is saying to the churches.

What is He saying to the global Church now?
What is the Spirit saying to the local congregation now?

---

4   Ramsay, *The Seven Letters*, 412.

What is He saying to you, right now?

As we take heed to both listen to Jesus and do what He's saying, may we find ourselves changed—from glory to glory—into His image.

And now, Father, may Your will be done in us as it is in heaven. Jesus, we look forward to Your return. Amen.

Before You Go

Whatever life looks like for you, I hope this book has encouraged you. My prayer is that you will have felt the presence of the Lord, and allowed Him to speak to you as you read through these pages. The only question remaining is: how will you respond?

Perhaps you are far from God today. Maybe you've heard about Jesus, but you've never known Him personally, never sought Him for forgiveness of sins, never fully given yourself to Him—your past, present, and future. Don't let today end without submitting your life to Jesus! Acknowledge your sins. Confess them to Him and He will forgive you and cleanse you. He gave His life for you, specifically, so that you could be spiritually born again and live a brand new life in Him.

Before you go—before you close the cover on this book—give your life to Jesus. Below you'll find a prayer that you can use as a model. I encourage you to pray something like it and then get connected with a local church to grow in your relationship with Jesus. It will be your very first step into a new life—an abundant life—in Him.

Father, I have sinned and come short of your glory. I am sorry and need your forgiveness. Please forgive all my sins, and wash my heart clean of any unrighteousness.

Jesus, thank you for giving your life for me. From this day on, I am committed to living my life for you.

Holy Spirit, I need your help. Please fill me, teach me, and empower me to live in such a way that is pleasing to You.

Lord, thank you for new life which I will live by faith in Jesus who loved me and gave Himself up for me.

Jesus, it's in your name I pray. Amen.

Bibliography

Monographs

Barclay, William. *The Revelation of John,* vol 1. Louisville, KY: Westminster John Knox Press, 1976.

Beale, G.K. The Book of Revelation: A Commentary of the Greek Text. Grand Rapids, MI: Wm. B. Eerdmans Publishing Co., 1999.

Beasley-Murray, George R. "Revelation," *New Bible Commentary: 21ˢᵗ Century Edition,* ed. D.A. Carson et al., 4th ed. Leicester, England; Downers Grove IL: Inter-Varsity Press, 1994.

Hays, J. Daniel. The Temple and the Tabernacle: A Study of God's Dwelling Places from Genesis to Revelation. Grand Rapids, MI: Baker Books, 2016.

Hemer, Colin J. *The Letters to the Seven Churches of Asia in Their Local Setting.* Grand Rapids, MI; Cambridge, U.K.; Livonia, MI: William B. Eerdmans Publishing Company; Dove Booksellers, 2001.

Hughes, Robert B., and J. Carl Laney, *Tyndale Concise Bible Commentary,* The Tyndale Reference Library. Weaton, IL: Tyndale House Publishers, 2001.

Jamieson, Robert, A. R. Fausset, and David Brown. *Commentary Critical and Explanatory on the Whole Bible,* vol. 2. Oak Harbor, WA: Logos Research Systems, Inc., 1997.

Morgan, G. Campbell. The Letters of Our Lord: A First Century Message to Twentieth Century Christians. London, U.K.: Pickering and Inglis LTD.

Osborne, Grant R. *Revelation,* Baker Exegetical Commentary on the New Testament. Grand Rapids, MI: Baker Academic, 2002.

Ramsay, W.M. The Letters to the Seven Churches of Asia and Their Place in the Plan of the Apocalypse. London: Hodder and Stoughton, 1904.

Stanley, Andy. *The Principle of the Path.* Nashville, TN: Thomas Nelson, 2008.

Westfall, Cynthia Long. Paul and Gender: Reclaiming the Apostle's Vision for Men and Women in Christ. Grand Rapids, MI: Baker Academic, 2016.

Wiersbe, Warren W. *The Bible Exposition Commentary*, vol. 2. Wheaton, IL: Victor Books, 1996.

Ancient Texts

Eusebius. *The History of the Church*, Translated by G. A. Williamson. London, England: Penguin Books, 1989.

Flavius Josephus. *The Works of Josephus: Complete and Unabridged*, Translated by William Whiston. Peabody: MI: Hendrickson Publishers, Inc., 2004.

Herodotus. *The Histories*, Translated by Tom Holland. New York, NY.: Penguin Books, 2015.

St. Irenaeus of Lyons. *Against Heresies*, Translated by Alexander Roberts. Jackson, MI: Ex Fontibus Company, 2020.

Tacitus. *The Annals*. University of Chicago. https://penelope.uchicago. edu/Thayer/E/Roman/Texts/Tacitus.

Articles and Websites

Kiliç, Murat. "The Roman Imperial Cult in Smyrna," *Belleten* 76, no. 276, 2012.

Kurtz, Ronni. "Why Are There So Many Angry Theologians?" *Christianity Today*, Jan. 3, 2023. https://www.christianitytoday.com/ct/2023/ januaryfebruary/book-awards-kurtz-fruitful-theology-angry-theologians.html

Suffield, Kittie L. "Little is Much When God is in It," 1924. Hymnary. https://hymnary.org/text/in_the_harvest_field_now_ripened.

"Modeling the Future of Religion in America." *Pew Research Center*, Washington, D.C. September 13, 2022. https://www.pewresearch. org/religion/2022/09/13/modeling-the-future-of-religion-in-america/

Worldometer. https://www.worldometers.info/coronavirus. Accessed November 9, 2022.

About the Author

J.F. Wright has been in ministry for over twenty-five years. He is currently serving as pastor of a church in a small town in California. Recently, he graduated from the University of California in Davis, earning degrees in English and History. "It's never too late to start something new."

Evergreen Faith is his first book.

Connect with the author on Twitter and Facebook:
@jfwrighter

Read more from the author on his Substack:
jfwrighter.substack.com

www.ingramcontent.com/pod-product-compliance
Lightning Source LLC
Chambersburg PA
CBHW060846120626
46553CB00013B/1985